**DATE DUE**

|  |  |  |  |
|--|--|--|--|
|  |  |  |  |
|  |  |  |  |
|  |  |  |  |
|  |  |  |  |
|  |  |  |  |
|  |  |  |  |
|  |  |  |  |
|  |  |  |  |
|  |  |  |  |
|  |  |  |  |
|  |  |  |  |
|  |  |  |  |
|  |  |  |  |
|  |  |  |  |
|  |  |  |  |
|  |  |  |  |
|  |  |  |  |
|  |  |  |  |
|  |  |  |  |

GAYLORD                    PRINTED IN U.S.A.

# A SAVAGE THUNDER

## ANTIETAM AND THE BLOODY ROAD TO FREEDOM

# JIM MURPHY

MARGARET K. McELDERRY BOOKS

New York   London   Toronto   Sydney

# ‡ 241304363 1/10

## ACKNOWLEDGMENTS

This book came together over the course of ten years. During that time I had the good fortune to work with a number of very knowledgeable individuals who generously helped me unearth information and collect the images that appear in this book. Special thanks are owed to: Janice Frye, Park Historian/Curator, Fredericksburg and Spotsylvania National Military Park; Melinda Gales, Photo Services Manager, the Museum of the Confederacy; Lizanne Garrett, the National Portrait Gallery, Smithsonian Institution; Clifton P. Hyatt, U.S. Army Military History Institute; Maja Keech, Reference Specialist, Prints and Photographs Division, the Library of Congress; Matthew Krogh, Research Assistant, Valentine Richmond History Center; Chris Kull, Archivist, Monroe County Historical Commission Archives; and Bryan McDaniel, Chicago History Museum.

## PHOTO CREDITS

The Library of Congress: iv–v, vii, viii, 2, 4, 6, 7, 9, 10, 11, 12, 15, 17, 18, 20, 23, 24, 26, 29, 30, 32, 33, 34–35, 37, 38, 39, 42, 44, 46, 48, 50, 52, 57, 59, 62, 64, 68, 71, 73, 74, 77, 78, 80, 81, 82–83, 87; The Century War Book: 16; Valentine Richmond History Center: 41; Fredericksburg and Spotsylvania National Military Park: 45; Author's Collection: 53; The Museum of the Confederacy: 55; Georgia Department of Archives and History: 60; Monroe County Historical Commission Archives: 63; Georgetown University Press: 70; The National Portrait Gallery: 84; Chicago History Museum: 88.

*Page iv: While shells explode and men are shot around them, Union troops march in formation past the Dunker Church.*

Margaret K. McElderry Books
An imprint of Simon & Schuster Children's Publishing Division
1230 Avenue of the Americas, New York, New York 10020
Copyright © 2009 by Jim Murphy
Book design by Patti Ratchford
The text for this book is set in Coldstyle.
Manufactured in China
10 9 8 7 6 5 4 3 2 1
Library of Congress Cataloging-in-Publication Data
Murphy, Jim, 1947–
A savage thunder : Antietam and the bloody road to freedom /
Jim Murphy.—1st ed.
p.   cm.
Includes bibliographical references and index.
ISBN: 978-0-689-87633-2 (hardcover)
1. Antietam, Battle of, Md., 1862—Juvenile literature. I. Title.
E474.65.M87 2009 973.7'336—dc22 2008032738

FIRST
EDITION

To Dr. David Blank—
an inquisitive individual, a genuine scholar, and a great father-in-law

# ✳ Contents ✳

# ✳ Preface ✳

"The present seems to be the [best] time since the commencement of the war for the Confederate Army to enter Maryland."
—A message from General Robert E. Lee, commander, Army of Northern Virginia, to Jefferson Davis, president, the Confederate States of America, September 3, 1862

"There is every probability that the enemy, baffled in his intended capture of Washington, will cross the Potomac, and make a raid into Maryland or Pennsylvania. A movable army must be immediately organized to meet him again in the field."
—Orders from Henry W. Halleck, general-in-chief of Union Armies, to General George B. McClellan, commander, Army of the Potomac, September 3, 1862

With these simple messages two great armies were set on a collision course that would end fourteen days later at Antietam Creek, just outside of Sharpsburg, Maryland. If we could ask any of the 140,000 soldiers composing these armies why they were willing to fight and possibly die, the overwhelming response from the men of both sides would have been remarkably similar: They were fighting for their freedom.

Jefferson Davis spoke for the Confederate side when he insisted the Civil War was declared to maintain "the political rights, the freedom, equality, and State sovereignty" won by our Revolutionary War forefathers. By "State sovereignty" Davis meant the right of every state to enact any laws it wanted. And if the federal government objected, the state could decide not to be a part of the United States.

"We all declare for *liberty*," the president of the United States, Abraham Lincoln, replied, "but in using the same *word* we do not mean the same *thing*." He then made clear that the conflict was necessary to "settle this question now . . . Whether in a free government the minority have the right to break up the government whenever they choose."

Whether to preserve the Union or not was certainly an important reason to fight. Our lives—indeed the lives of people around the world—would be quite different now had the South succeeded in separating itself from the United States. But nowhere during the first year and a half of the war did this talk about fighting for freedom and liberty include mention of the real reason for the war: the enslavement of four and a half million African-American men, women, and children.

*In 1863 a weary Abraham Lincoln sat for this photograph in his White House office.*

It was, at best, hypocritical for both sides to send soldiers into combat without addressing this issue honestly. Lincoln, for instance, came under heavy criticism, both from those opposed to slavery and from political opponents, for his lack of candor. One prominent African-American leader, Frederick Douglass, pointed out the obvious: "To fight against slaveholders, without fighting against slavery, is but a half-hearted business. . . . War for the destruction of liberty must be met with war for the destruction of slavery." Yet even as casualties mounted and the criticism heated up, Lincoln refused to make the conflict a war against slavery.

All of this changed when a series of surprising Confederate victories in 1862 left the Union armies dazed and demoralized and put the very existence of the United States in doubt. By July, Lincoln had come to realize that the emancipation of the slaves was "absolutely essential to the preservation of the Union. . . ."

As the Confederate and Union armies marched toward each other, very few of the men realized that the idea of freedom—and with it the nature of the war—was about to change. Nor did they know they were going to take part in an epic battle that would prove to be the bloodiest single day in American history.

*The first Confederate troops began crossing the Potomac before sunrise on the morning of September 5.*
*Union soldiers in the foreground would fire a few shots, then head back to camp to report what they had seen.*

# ✳ 1 ✳
# Invasion

---

Cheer, boys, cheer, we'll march away to battle,
Cheer, boys, cheer, for our sweethearts and our wives,
Cheer, boys, cheer, we'll nobly do our duty.
—"The Southern Boys" by Henry Russell, 1861

———◆———

On Friday, September 5, 1862, the rattle of drums accompanied by sharp, insistent bugle notes summoned the Confederate army to march. The heavy tramp of boots and clomping of horse's hooves on the dry dirt road soon had clouds of dust swirling in the warm air. An hour later the lead brigade of General Robert E. Lee's Army of Northern Virginia reached the banks of the Potomac River.

The 10th Virginia was the first to enter the water at White's Ford. In places, the water was waist-high, and many men removed their boots and trousers to keep them dry during the half mile journey. "Never did I behold so many naked legs in my life," recalled Private Draughton Stith Haynes.

Crossing with the troops were hundreds and hundreds of wagons carrying food, equipment, and ammunition, most driven by African-American slaves. Several wagons became stuck in the mud and had to be pushed free by grumbling drivers. Mules refused to leave the cool water and were "cussed" onto the opposite shore of Maryland.

When the lead brigade's musicians finally scrambled ashore, they formed up into a neat line and played "Maryland! My Maryland!" Soldiers cheered loudly when they heard the melody and could be heard singing above the teamsters' curses and officers' shouted orders:

"The despot's heel is on thy shore,
Maryland!
His torch is at thy temple door,
Maryland!

Avenge the patriotic gore
That flecked the streets of Baltimore,
And be the battle queen of yore,
Maryland! My Maryland!"

As he approached the ford, Sergeant James Shinn was amazed by what he saw. The golden autumn sun "caused the rippled surface [of the water] to sparkle with the brilliancy of a sea of silver studded with diamonds

set in dancing beds of burnished gold. . . . The scene was one of grand & magnificent interest."

More shouts accompanied Robert E. Lee as he came to the ford, though his mood was markedly more somber. The logistics of safely moving an army of 75,000 men, plus all their baggage, supplies, equipment, and horses, across a river and into enemy territory was a nightmare of details. Plus Lee had to shoulder the knowledge that in the days ahead, his every decision could mean life or death for the cheering men around him.

If this was not burden enough, Lee was enduring great pain as the result of a freak accident. Several days before, he had fallen while trying to restrain his horse and suffered injuries to his hands. Because both were now encased in clumsy wood splints, Lee wasn't able to hold the reins of his horse to ride across the river. Instead, his rather inglorious crossing into Maryland was accomplished while riding inside an army ambulance.

For several days after this, Lee's army continued to make the trip across the Potomac accompanied by excited cheers and lively music. General Lee referred to this march as nothing more than an "expedition." It was, in fact, a bold campaign that would take the brutal Civil War to the North. Its aim was just as monumental: to destroy the North's will to fight and thus gain complete independence for the South.

Lee knew this was the perfect time to invade Maryland and harass the enemy capital at Washington. Since the beginning of the Civil War in 1861, most of the hard fighting had taken place in the South, much of it in his home state of Virginia. He wanted to move the fighting—and hundreds of thousands of hungry Union and Confederate soldiers—off the exhausted land.

Farmers in Maryland owned tens of thousands of horses, cows, cattle, and pigs. They harvested millions of bushels of wheat and corn every year and their orchards were lush with fruit. Lee's army could live off this bounty for months, all the while allowing Virginia to recuperate from nearly a year and a half of terrible fighting.

But there was more to the invasion than finding food. Until June 1862, the Union army had seemed to be in control of the war. General George McClellan had launched his Peninsula Campaign in March of that year, landing the Army of the Potomac at Fortress Monroe on the tip of the Virginia peninsula and marching it to within five miles of the Confederate capital at Richmond. While this was happening, a fleet of twenty-four federal warships under the command of Admiral David Farragut had taken control of the Mississippi River and pounded away at the city of Vicksburg, Mississippi, with over 245 pieces of artillery. Union troops also held strong positions in Mississippi, Tennessee, and Kentucky, and were threatening to cut off needed enemy supplies.

This series of Union successes took the South by surprise and dampened the spirit of rebellion. "Reverse after reverse comes in quick succession," lamented the *Richmond Dispatch.* "We have nothing but disaster." When Fort Donelson in Tennessee and its garrison of 14,000 soldiers surrendered to Union forces, the vice president of the Confederacy, Alexander Stephens, told a friend, "The Confederacy is lost."

Then everything began to change.

Vicksburg refused to surrender despite several weeks of nonstop bombardment. Eventually, a frustrated Farragut took his fleet and retreated downriver. Next, Confederate raiders struck at superior Union forces in Kentucky at Munfordville and Richmond, capturing more than 8,000 soldiers. Then, after four months of steadily advancing,

*General Robert E. Lee, commander of the Army of North Virginia.*

McClellan's Peninsula Campaign stalled with Richmond in sight. Despite outnumbering the enemy by 50,000 soldiers, McClellan took heavy losses in a series of brutal battles and decided to withdraw his army from Virginia. Following this, 24,000 Confederate troops under Thomas "Stonewall" Jackson crushed another Union army led by General John Pope at Cedar Mountain, Virginia. Three weeks later, Pope received another sound thrashing at the Battle of Second Manassas and was in full retreat by August 31.

As September began, the Union army had withdrawn from many key locations and had pulled back to where it had been more than a year earlier. A thoroughly disgusted Lieutenant Charles Brewster complained, "We have fought more desperately, lost more men, and endured more hardships than any army under the sun, and all for nothing."

The collapse of the Union armies was so complete that the *New York Times* fretted, "The Country is in . . . extreme peril. The Rebels seem to be pushing forward their forces all along the border line from the Atlantic to the Missouri." Unless Lee's troops could be stopped, predicted the *Chicago Times*, "the Union cause is doomed to a speedy and disastrous overthrow."

The time was right, Lee had told Confederate President Jefferson Davis when he proposed his plan to invade the North. Harass and frighten Washington enough, maybe even score a victory or two on the battlefield, and the demoralized people of the North might pressure their elected officials into allowing the Southern states to secede. Even if that did not happen, Lee hoped an aggressive campaign could still produce another important result.

Since the war's beginning, the South had hoped that

England, France, and other European countries would recognize the Confederacy as a legitimate government. When this happened, the South expected that its new allies would send them needed aid in the form of money and arms. In addition, they hoped the Europeans would urge the federal government to negotiate a settlement to the Civil War, one that would mean Confederate independence.

To push Europe to do this, the South had halted the export of cotton to foreign countries, though they cleverly blamed the resulting shortages on an official Union blockade of Southern shipping. The cotton famine and mill closings that followed had put a severe strain on a number of European economies. In England, for instance, 85,000 mill workers were out of jobs because of the lack of cotton, while another 350,000 were earning half of what they had before the outbreak of the Civil War.

As summer was drawing to a close in 1862, both England and France were on the verge of recognizing the Confederate States as a separate and independent nation. The French monarch, Napoleon III, had gone so far as to tell the Confederate envoy to his court that the "accounts of the defeat of the Federal armies from Richmond [had convinced him that the] re-establishment of the Union [is] impossible." Three day later he sent a telegram to his foreign minister in London that read: "Ask the English government if it does not believe the time has come to recognize the South."

The chief stumbling block to this was slavery. Neither England nor France endorsed the South's use of slave labor, Britain having abolished it in 1833 and France in 1848. Because most ordinary citizens in Europe were strongly antislavery, the English and French governments did not want to appear to be condoning such a repugnant institution. Lee hoped that the financial crisis caused by the shortage of cotton, plus a successful campaign in the North, would compel these European powers to overlook their moral objections and act out of economic self-interest.

The politics of the war were not on the mind of General J. E. B. (Jeb) Stuart as he led 1,500 cavalry troopers across the Potomac. He had a job to perform. As soon as he had his men in Maryland, he headed south at a gallop toward Washington. He then turned up a country road leading to a tiny town named Poolesville, where he encountered the first Union resistance. The 100 Union soldiers put up a brief, spirited fight, then realized they were vastly outnumbered, and scampered. But Stuart had accomplished what he'd set out to do. The fleeing Union soldiers would spread word that the rebel army was heading for the capital, possibly causing citizens and nervous politicians to panic and flee.

While Stuart's men were creating a noisy diversion, the rest of Lee's men and the thousands of slaves who drove the wagons, shoed the horses, cooked the food, and did other chores were marching away from Washington, following the tow path of the C&O Canal toward the Monocacy River. This was no spit-and-polish army either. Their uniforms—what there was of them—were little better than tattered rags; most faces were unwashed and unshaven, while unkempt, knotted hair tumbled from under battered slouch hats. "They were the dirtiest men I ever saw," recalled a boy named Leighton Parks as he watched the men passing his home, "a most ragged, lean, and hungry set of wolves."

They were more than just hungry; they were ravenous. Unfortunately, the citizens in the area they

*Many very young boys entered military service as drummer boys, only to pick up a rifle during battle to fight alongside their older comrades.*

apple butter, bread, etc., got as many apples as I could carry, had a long chat with a pretty nice cross-eyed girl. I never saw apple butter until I came to Maryland. I am fond of it."

Still, the largest number of soldiers had to resort to foraging for their suppers. Foraging meant taking whatever food a soldier could find, even if it was unripe corn or sour green apples. Because Lee had made it very clear that he would not tolerate stealing by any of his officers or soldiers, some imaginative stories were invented to explain the sudden appearance of a meal. "Some men came into camp one morning with a pig," explained artillerist George W. Shere with as straight a face as he could manage. "[They] declared that the pig attacked them, and they were obliged to kill it in self defense. It was keenly enjoyed for breakfast and no questions asked."

On the first night of the invasion a tired but jubilant Southern army made camp with bellies full. They had taken the war to the north and had encountered little serious resistance. "As I am writing," noted a member of the horse artillery, George Neese, "I hear soldiers shouting, huzzahing all around us." A company band began to play a rousing tune, "to swell the cheer of the merry throng." The day had gone so perfectly that it didn't seem as if anything could stop the invasion.

were marching through were strongly for the Union and greeted their uninvited guests with a mixture of cool reserve, curiosity, and resignation. One farmer, when told his fence rails were going to be used for cooking fires, sighed and said, "Burn away. That's what rails are for when there's no other wood around."

Because there was no spontaneous rush by citizens to feed troops, several commanders had to purchase entire fields of corn for their men. Soldiers whose officers could not afford to buy them dinner had to get their supplies from willing farmers. J. R. Boulware, a surgeon from South Carolina, wrote in his diary: "I bought some

# ✴ 2 ✴
# Panic

---

"The rebels are coming," far and near
Rang the tidings of dread and fear;
Some paled, and cowered, and sought to hide;
Some stood erect in their fearless pride;
And women shuddered, and children cried.

—"The Ballad of Ishmael Day" by Elizabeth Akers Allen, 1865

obert E. Lee and his army might have been even more confident had they known what was happening in Washington.

The series of Confederate victories and the dramatic shift in the momentum of the war had completely unsettled both politicians and civilians in the city. Concern grew when Lee crossed the Potomac. Was he going to strike at Washington, DC? people wondered. Or at Baltimore? Or maybe even at Philadelphia?

That the shattered remnants of Pope's army began staggering into the city in early September only added to the sense of unease. The general-in-chief of all Union military operations, Henry W. Halleck, did not help to calm nerves when he banned newspaper reporters from interviewing these soldiers. News-hungry reporters simply wandered through military camps situated around Washington and reported every rumor they heard as fact. One suggested that General Lee had been spotted behind Union lines. Another had Jeb Stuart's cavalry poised to attack Alexandria, Virginia, which was only five miles south of the capital.

The feeling of doom was heightened by the feverish activity to bolster the city's defenses. Large numbers of recently recruited soldiers were paraded through the crowded streets and stationed at entrances to the city; gunboats were brought up the Potomac and positioned to blast away when the enemy appeared on the opposite shore. When government workers were issued rifles and ammunition in preparation for a last ditch stand, residents began streaming out of town in carriages and on horseback. "Impressment into the [Confederate] ranks as common soldiers," wrote Dr. Lewis H. Steiner, "or [confinement] in a *Southern* prison—these were not attractive prospects for quiet, Union-loving citizens!"

*In order to protect Washington, DC, numerous forts were hastily constructed. This one guards one of the bridges leading into the city.*

*Right: General George B. McClellan, commander of the Army of the Potomac, and his wife, Ellen. His letters to her reveal his distaste and loathing for many of the people he had to report to, including Abraham Lincoln.*

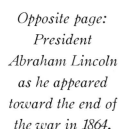

*Opposite page: President Abraham Lincoln as he appeared toward the end of the war in 1864.*

Meanwhile, clerks at the War Department loaded important documents onto wagons and hurried them north to safety. The steamship *Wachusett* was kept ready at all times, its boilers hot, poised to spirit away important government officials should the city come under bombardment.

Things were even more chaotic inside the War Department. Following the rout of Pope's army, President Abraham Lincoln, Secretary of War Edwin Stanton, and General-in-Chief Halleck had come to a decision.

What remained of Pope's army would be combined with McClellan's for the defense of Washington. The only question was who would command this force.

Pope had so botched his campaign that no one considered him fit to command. But similar misgivings were felt about McClellan as well.

On numerous occasions both Halleck and Lincoln had ordered McClellan to rush troops to Pope's aid. But McClellan had steadfastly refused to do so, coming up with one feeble excuse after another for his inactivity. According to the president's private secretary, John Hay, Lincoln believed that McClellan "wanted Pope defeated." Lincoln saw "a design, a purpose, in breaking down Pope, without regard to the consequences to the country."

Other senior officers in the army, plus most of the president's cabinet, agreed. A petition was drawn up urging the president to dismiss McClellan immediately and bring him before a military court for failure to follow orders. Lincoln did not disagree with his advisors, but he still did not relieve McClellan of command.

McClellan was a lot of annoying things. He was arrogant, imperious, self-involved, and disdainful of all of Lincoln's advisors, most other senior army officers, and especially of Lincoln, calling him "an idiot . . . nothing more than a well-meaning baboon." McClellan firmly believed that God had placed him on earth to do great things, and heaven help anyone who stood in his way.

And he had indeed refused to reinforce Pope, thus dooming hundreds of soldiers to an early grave. In a letter to his wife, Ellen, he had predicted that Pope "will be badly thrashed within two days . . . very badly whipped he will be & ought to be . . ." Once this "villain" was humiliated and out of the way, McClellan expected that Lincoln and his cronies "will be very glad to turn over the redemption of their affairs to me."

Lincoln would have gladly sacked his deceptive young commander. In fact, he offered the command of the army to the highly respected General Ambrose Burnside. Burnside was an amiable, robust man with truly memorable muttonchop sideburns. He was also keenly aware of his limitations as a military leader and turned down the offer politely, explaining, "I had always unreservedly expressed that I was not competent to command such a large army as this."

This left Lincoln without many choices. He had heard that Union soldiers had lost the will to fight. One officer fresh from the Peninsula Campaign found himself "sorrowful and humiliated when looking back over a year and finding ourselves on the same ground as then. The debris of the Grand Army [has] come back to its starting place with ranks decimated, its morale failing, while thousands who sleep their last sleep on the Peninsula demand the cause of their sacrifice."

Lieutenant Charles Francis Adams Jr. looked at the beaten soldiers around him and wrote, "our army seems in danger of utter demoralization and I have not since the war began felt such a tug on my nerves. . . . Everything is ripe for terrible panic."

Abraham Lincoln knew such an army would not put up much of a fight against Lee's army. He knew something else as well. For all of his faults, McClellan—known fondly as Little Mac among his men—was beloved by his troops and could rally them behind him.

With sad resignation, the president had to admit that only George McClellan could "reorganize the army and bring it out of chaos. McClellan has the army with him [and] we must use the tools we have. There is no

*African Americans were also used by the Union Army, often receiving room and meals as pay. This watercolor shows them providing the muscle to hoist a cannon into position.*

man [who can] lick these troops of ours into shape half as well as he. . . ." To the shock of everyone in his cabinet Lincoln announced that George McClellan would be commander of the army that would defend Washington from attack.

Another issue was troubling Lincoln as well. On his desk was the draft of a document he'd been working on since early July: the Emancipation Proclamation.

Since the beginning of the Civil War, abolitionists had insisted that the war should be fought to outlaw slavery. Lincoln abhorred slavery and wanted it banned from the United States, but he had resisted making slavery a direct target of the war because of practical concerns.

At the time, the Constitution of the United States stated that slavery was legal. As president he was sworn to uphold the Constitution; therefore he couldn't legally wage war on slavery, no matter what his personal feelings were. More important, he worried that the border states of Delaware, Maryland, Missouri, and Kentucky, which supported the Union and in which slavery was still legal, would switch sides if he made abolition a war goal.

Finally, he was genuinely concerned that many of his officers and soldiers might leave the army if they felt they were fighting to abolish slavery. McClellan, for one, had stated numerous times that if the South returned to the Union the institution of slavery would be "religiously respected." To a friend McClellan wrote, "Help me to dodge the [negro]—we want nothing to do with him. I am fighting to preserve the integrity of the Union and the power of the Govt—on no other issue." Faced with the real possibility of a military revolt, Lincoln made it clear from the beginning that preserving the United States was the goal of the war.

But as the war dragged along and casualties mounted, slavery began to be seen as a military necessity for the South. Slave labor raised the crops that fed rebel forces and their horses. Slaves planted and picked the cotton that was then sold to buy weapons. Slaves dug trenches, drove wagons, cooked meals, and did many other important military chores. In one Alabama factory producing ammunition, 310 of the 400 workers were slaves. All of this African-American labor freed white Confederate men to fight against the North. "Why? Oh! Why, in the name of all that is rational," declared Frederick Douglass, "does our Government allow its enemies this powerful advantage? The very stomach of the rebellion is the negro in the condition of a slave. Arrest that hoe in the hands of the negro, and you smite rebellion in the very seat of its life."

When Congress passed the Confiscation Acts in 1862, they granted the president the power to seize any property that might be of use to the enemy armies. Lincoln's Emancipation Proclamation was therefore a cautious step to eliminate slavery by classifying it as a military problem.

"And, as a fit and necessary military measure," read his proclamation's final line, "all persons held as slaves within any state or states, wherein the constitutional authority of the United States shall not then be practically recognized, submitted to, and maintained, shall then, thenceforward, and forever, be free."

The Proclamation set January 1, 1863, as the date when it would take effect. The president was therefore offering a carrot to the Confederate states. Stop the war, return to the Union, and slavery would still exist (at least until Congress addressed the issue again). Continue the rebellion and the South would lose forever what it believed was its most important economic asset.

Lincoln read the Emancipation Proclamation to his cabinet on July 22. There was general approval of the measure on moral and military grounds, but several cabinet members had questions. The most important came from Secretary of State William H. Seward. Because of the recent string of military disasters suffered by the Union armies, he worried that such a move might be viewed as a desperate attempt to have slaves revolt against their owners or, as he put it, "our last shriek on the retreat."

Sadly, Lincoln had to agree. He put the document in his desk and decided to wait until he could make the announcement from a position of strength. That meant waiting for something positive to happen on the field of battle.

McClellan, Lincoln was sure, could whip his men into fighting condition. But he was not at all certain his general could lead them to victory.

# ★ 3 ★
# Onwards

Forth from its scabbard, pure and bright,
Flashed the sword of Lee!
Far in the front of the deadly fight,
High o'er the brave in the cause of Right
Its stainless sheen, like a beacon light,
Led us to Victory!
—"The Sword of Robert Lee" by Abram Joseph Ryan, 1897

Lee got his army across the Potomac and occupied the town of Frederick on the seventh of September without firing a shot. As his men marched, they blew up railroad bridges and cut telegraph lines, all in an effort to disrupt Union communications.

Lee had hoped that entering Maryland, a slave state, would prompt many of its residents to join Confederate troops in the fight. But the reception given them in Frederick was decidedly cold. One annoyed resident told the *Baltimore American*, "I have never seen a mass of such filthy, strong-smelling men. . . . They were the roughest set of creatures I ever saw, their features, hair, and clothing matted with dirt and filth; and the scratching they kept up gave warrant to vermin in abundance."

Prior to the invasion, Southern newspapers had predicted that as many as 50,000 Maryland citizens would rally to the cause and fight the Union. An embarrassed Lee told President Davis that at most he thought he might get a few hundred volunteers. "I do not anticipate," he said, almost by way of apology, "any general rising of the people in our behalf."

Another problem he encountered was straggling by his soldiers. Stragglers were men who were supposed to be with their units but had left the line of march without permission. Lee considered these men cowards "who desert their comrades in peril" and "unworthy members of an army that has immortalized itself."

No doubt some of these stragglers had gone missing because they wanted to avoid battle or were trying to steal and cook dinner. But most were simply exhausted. Lee's men had been fighting without rest and without adequate food or medical attention for nearly ten weeks. Furthermore, their recent diet of green apples and unripe corn had produced thousands of cases of debilitating diarrhea.

*Both armies had foragers whose job it was to round up food from local farmers. Here one crew has just gotten dinner for the night and are setting off for the next farm down the road.*

As a result, of the 75,000 soldiers who had crossed the Potomac, nearly 10,000 were wandering aimlessly through the countryside, sick and unable to keep up with their comrades.

But there had been encouraging news as well. Word had reached Lee that McClellan had been reappointed commander of the Union forces and specifically charged to defend the federal capital. Lee had studied McClellan's operations carefully during the Peninsula Campaign and felt he knew his opponent well, something that would influence all subsequent decisions of his invasion.

He made this clear to General John G. Walker as the two stood before a large map. Lee, his hands still in splints, nodded his head toward Harrisburg, Pennsylvania, and said, "That is the objective of the campaign."

He intended to destroy the railroad bridge at Harrisburg and cut the Union line of supply. "After that," Lee went on, "I can turn my attention to Philadelphia, Baltimore, or Washington, as may seem best for our interests."

Walker was astonished by the audacity of the plan, and when Lee noticed this, he asked if Walker knew McClellan. Walker had met him several years before, but didn't really know much about his military skills. "He is an able general but a very cautious one," Lee told Walker. "His enemies among his own people think him too much so. His army is in a very demoralized and chaotic condition, and will not be prepared for offensive operations— or he will not think so—for three or four weeks."

Those weeks would allow Lee to reach Harrisburg and the train bridge. Then he would hunt for the perfect place to battle McClellan, an area with terrain that suited the Confederate army's ability to move and maneuver quickly.

But before the plan could be put into effect, Lee had to deal with the federal garrison at Harper's Ferry, West Virginia.

Harper's Ferry was located where the Shenandoah and Potomac Rivers met and was surrounded by steep, high hills. The federals had 10,500 men there at the time, a number that would swell to over 13,000 when another nearby post joined them several days later. Most of these troops were recent recruits with little training and no battle experience, while their commander, Colonel Dixon Miles, was known to spend most of his days dead drunk.

Lee wanted Harper's Ferry because it sat at the northern end of the Shenandoah Valley, a corridor he had to control in order to get supplies of food and ammunition.

Lee decided to gamble based on his opponent's cautiousness. On September 9, he issued Special Orders No. 191 that divided up his army into four parts.

Stonewall Jackson would lead the largest number of soldiers across the Potomac to attack Harper's Ferry from the west, while two other divisions would strike at the garrison from the south and east. Two-thirds of the Army of Northern Virginia would be involved in this operation. Lee expected that the commander of the federal troops would surrender as soon as he realized that he was trapped and outnumbered. Meanwhile, Lee would take the remaining troops through a series of rugged mountain gaps and wait to reunite with Jackson and the other divisions near Hagerstown.

Seven copies of Special Orders No. 191 were written out, and messengers rode off to deliver them to the commanders involved in the operation. On September 10, Lee's army split up and marched out of Frederick. They were in a buoyant, eager-to-fight mood. "Just now," wrote Major Walter Taylor to his wife, Mary Lou, "it does appear as if God [is] truly with us. All along our lines the movement is onward."

*An 1862 view of Harper's Ferry and the railroad bridge. Its location and railroad connections made Harper's Ferry an important shipping location of supplies and troops.*

*Union soldiers loved Little Mac. Here a group sings a popular song of the time, "McClellan Is Our Man."*

# ★ 4 ★
# S.O. 191

One noonday, at my window in town,
I saw a sight—saddest that eyes can see—
Young soldiers marching lustily
Unto the wars,
With fifes, and flags in mottoed pageantry;
While all the porches, walks, and doors
Were rich with ladies cheering royally.
—"Ball's Bluff" by Herman Melville, 1861

Early on September 2, a somber Abraham Lincoln and Henry Halleck walked several blocks to McClellan's house, where they found him having breakfast. There the two older men asked McClellan to take charge of what was left of Pope's army, plus the new recruits flooding into Washington, and meld them with his army into a single unit.

McClellan wasted no time in crowing about his "victory" over his critics. "Again I have been called upon to save the country," he boasted to Ellen, a chore he would undertake because "under the circumstances no one else *could* save the country."

For all of his bombast and ego, McClellan spent the days following his reappointment in a whirl of activity. His first move was to reorganize the chain of command for the army. Commanders were told to have their men ready to march immediately with three days' rations. Next, stragglers were rounded up and sent to their proper units, while wagonloads of food and other needed supplies were once again set in motion. Two days later, ten thousand troops had been redeployed in a strong defensive arc several miles outside of Washington.

McClellan spent these days rallying his troops as well. He rode from camp to camp on his black horse, waving his cap to greet startled soldiers. As soon as word spread that Little Mac was on the road, the cheering began. "From extreme sadness we passed in a twinkling to a delirium of delight," recalled William H. Powell. "A Deliverer had come. . . . Men threw their caps high into the air, and danced and frolicked like schoolboys."

*A long line of Union stragglers being led to headquarters.*

Stephen Weld wrote to his father that "Every one felt happy and jolly. We felt there was some chance. . . . The effect of this man's presence . . . was electrical. . . ."

A reporter who did not like McClellan very much saw the soldiers' spontaneous outpouring of enthusiasm for their commander and wrote, "I have disbelieved the reports of the army's affection for McClellan, being entirely unable to account for the phenomenon, [and] I cannot account for it to my satisfaction now, but I accept it as a fact."

Even McClellan was caught up in the excitement. In another letter to Ellen he was not bashful at all about telling her, "I hear them calling out to me as I ride among them, 'George, don't leave us again!'"

On September 7, McClellan moved his headquarters to Rockville, Maryland, some twenty miles from Washington. Approximately 85,000 men under arms moved out with him, while 72,500 troops were left behind to defend the city.

As with the Confederate army, hundreds of African Americans accompanied the Union forces. None of them were soldiers, however. Fearing that many whites would refuse to fight alongside African Americans, Lincoln and the War Department had expressly forbidden their enlistment as soldiers. But, like its Southern counterpart, the Union army found many uses for African Americans, whether they were former slaves from the South or freemen from the North. As General Ulysses S. Grant put it, "I have no hobby of my own with regards to the Negro, either to effect his freedom or to continue his bondage. . . . I am using them as teamsters, hospital attendants, company cooks and so forth, thus saving soldiers to carry the musket."

McClellan had organized and moved his army faster than anyone had anticipated, but he was still moving cautiously. In part, this was McClellan's nature. He was genuinely fond of the men under his command and did not like to engage them in battle unless he was absolutely certain he held a numerical superiority. Unfortunately, the information he received regarding Confederate troop strength was almost always incorrect.

During the Peninsula Campaign, he had received detailed intelligence reports from Allan Pinkerton, founder of the famed Pinkerton Detective Agency in Chicago. Pinkerton's agents tended to accept rumor and gossip as fact and reported them as highly reliable, which Pinkerton then sent along to McClellan without qualification. During the Peninsula Campaign, for instance, McClellan was convinced that he was facing 200,000 Confederate troops when in reality they numbered just over 75,000. As a result, McClellan always delayed engaging the enemy in battle, claiming he needed additional troops. Lincoln had a simple way to explain McClellan's reluctance to engage the enemy; he said Little Mac had developed a case of "the slows."

When he reached Rockville, McClellan had no real idea where the enemy was or how many he might have to face. He dispatched cavalry units to probe the countryside for information and soon received alarming reports of enemy troop movements in many areas. Stuart's lightning-quick cavalry had split into numerous smaller units and were circling the back roads and farm lanes, spreading false reports about their army's numbers and challenging any Union force that approached.

On the eleventh, McClellan telegraphed Halleck that the "entire rebel army . . . amounting to not less than 120,000 men, is in the vicinity of Frederick City." The soldiers were all veterans led by the South's best generals, he went on, and they intended "to hazard all upon the issue of the coming battle. They are probably aware that their forces are numerically superior to ours by at least 25 per cent." Before he could take on "the gigantic rebel army before us," McClellan told his superior, he needed reinforcements.

Despite feeling frustrated that McClellan was once again stalling, Halleck sent him 5,000 additional troops and promised to send more when he could. He also urged McClellan to rush to the aid of the Harper's Ferry garrison before Confederate troops got there.

McClellan did not rush anywhere, of course. He had split his army into three units and was moving them slowly forward along three separate parallel routes. On the eleventh, they were in a twenty-five-mile-wide arc just fifteen miles shy of Frederick.

Not only was he convinced that the enemy outnumbered him and had more experienced troops and commanding generals, he had absolutely no idea where they were headed. They might be going to Baltimore or up into Pennsylvania, but he couldn't rule out a countermarch that would let them attack Washington while he was out looking for them in the Maryland hills.

Lee had already split up his army and pulled most

of his troops out of Frederick, leaving behind a small squad to report when the Union army appeared. On Saturday the twelfth, an advance unit of Federal infantry finally entered town. There was a brief skirmish in which several soldiers were injured and one Union officer was captured, before the rebel soldiers withdrew and surrendered the town.

The town greeted the arriving Union troops with a jubilant welcome. "Handkerchiefs are waved, flags are thrown from Union houses, and a new life appears infused into the people," a resident wrote in his journal.

Citizens brought out food for their deliverers, while buckets of cider and whiskey were left along the road for thirsty soldiers. The crowd's enthusiasm charged the arriving soldiers with renewed energy. "The feelings and appearance of the men" seemed to change, noted a regimental surgeon. "The sallowness of face has given place to flush, the grumbling dissatisfaction to joyous hilarity, the camp at night, even after our marches, resounds with mirth and music."

Captain Oliver Wendell Holmes Jr. had fought in the Peninsula Campaign and was overjoyed to be clear of the swamps and bad luck he'd encountered there. "All of us feel a deuced sight more like a fight than in that forlorn Peninsula." This was a sentiment echoed by a soldier from Michigan. "I am willing to fight as long as there is a man left in the 2nd Regt before I see the North invaded."

While McClellan basked in the patriotic glow at Frederick, Lee established his headquarters in Hagerstown. He left Stuart's rear guard to defend the National Road through the Catoctin Mountains, and about 2,500 men to hold the same road through Turner's Gap in South Mountain.

Meanwhile, his offensive against Harper's Ferry was going slowly. Colonel Miles knew he was trapped, knew he hadn't a ghost of a chance, but simply refused to surrender.

Miles may have decided to hold on because he'd received messages telling him a large relief force was on the way. He may have also felt that to surrender would be another black mark on his already soiled military record. When asked by one of his officers if it might be better to pull out of town, he replied gruffly, "I am ordered by General Wool to hold this place, and God damn my soul to hell if I don't hold it against the enemy."

Miles's defense of Harper's Ferry was inept in almost every way. He never, for instance, put more than a few hundred soldiers in the mountains overlooking his garrison, thus allowing the Confederates to place artillery there. In fact, he bungled his command so badly that many people back in Washington thought it amounted to treason. But his stand forced Jackson and the two other attacking columns to put together a coordinated siege, a time-consuming operation that threw Robert E. Lee's schedule off by two whole days. During that period, Lee's entire army was scattered all over Maryland and extremely vulnerable to the approaching Union forces.

Many important moments in history are determined by small actions and chance. On the morning of September 13, as Union troops were pouring into Frederick, the 27th Indiana Infantry came to a farm just outside of town and halted to rest.

Corporal Barton Mitchell and a friend went off to rest their weary feet in the shade of a tree. As he was leaning back against a wood fence to relax, Mitchell noticed something in the tall grass nearby. It turned out

to be a rolled-up piece of paper with three cigars inside.

While his buddy went off to find matches so they could smoke the cigars, Mitchell glanced at the paper. At the top was written: "Headquarters, Army of North Virginia, Special Orders, No. 191."

Mitchell glanced at what was written below and later remembered that "As I read, each line became more interesting. I forgot those cigars." He knew he'd found something extremely important because the document was filled with the names of prominent Confederate generals and signed, "R.H. Chilton, Assist. Adj.-Gen. By command of Gen. R.E. Lee."

The document was rushed up the chain of command until it reached Colonel Samuel E. Pittman, at division headquarters. By sheer coincidence, Pittman had known Chilton before the war and recognized his handwriting.

Shortly before noon a messenger handed S.O. 191 to McClellan, whose eyes must have widened as it became clear what he held in his hands. His enemy had handed him their entire marching orders.

When McClellan finished reading what have come to be called the Lost Orders, he looked around at the men assembled there. "Now I know what to do!" he exclaimed. "Here is a paper with which if I cannot whip 'Bobbie Lee,' I will be willing to go home."

Then the ecstatic commander rushed off a telegraph message to Abraham Lincoln: "I think Lee has made a gross mistake, and that he will be severely punished for it. . . . I have all the plans of the rebels, and will catch them in their own trap. . . . My respects to Mrs. Lincoln." Then in an excited postscript, McClellan boasted, "Will send you trophies."

The fighting at Fox's Gap on South Mountain. The wounded man (to the left)
being attended to by two men is Lieutenant Colonel Rutherford Hayes,
who would become president of the United States in 1878.

# ★ 5 ★
# The Gaps

Where are you going, soldiers,
With banners, gun, and sword?
We're marching south to Canaan
To battle for the Lord!
—"To Canaan" by Oliver Wendell Holmes Sr., 1862

Despite knowing that Lee had divided up his army, McClellan remained cautious. S.O. 191 did not mention troop strength, so Little Mac continued to believe the forces just ahead with Lee still outnumbered him by 40,000 men (when in fact his troops outnumbered Lee's by that number). From the time he read S.O. 191, it took him six hours before he issued his first orders and Union soldiers did not begin marching for eighteen hours. Had he struck sooner, McClellan would have taken Lee by complete surprise, driven a wedge between his scattered army, and probably been able to aid the men at Harper's Ferry.

Lee had no idea his plans had been discovered, but he was wary of his opponent and nervous that it was taking longer than expected to capture Harper's Ferry. Then a bit of luck came his way. When McClellan was reading the Lost Orders, a Maryland citizen sympathetic to the South happened to be present. This unidentified spy immediately left Frederick and made his way through both lines to tell Jeb Stuart what he had witnessed. Stuart, in turn, informed Lee.

Lee acted quickly, anticipating a Union drive through the mountains. He sent a mounted courier to tell rear guard troops still in the South Mountains to hold on while he ordered additional troops to march back to reinforce them. Next, Stuart's men in the Catoctin Mountains were hurried back to the South Mountain area.

The Battle of South Mountain was actually three separate battles fought on September 14. At Turner's Gap on the National Road two engagements occurred. On the morning of the fourteenth, General Daniel Harvey (D. H.) Hill had between 7,000 and 8,000 Confederate soldiers available to stop the Union advance, and no cavalry to scout the enemy's route of march. This was important because there were actually four separate gaps through the mountain and he had to fan his men out over five miles to cover them all.

*Even a small piece of artillery required six horses and at least six men to transport and operate.*

At nine o'clock, isolated regiments of Union soldiers ran into the Confederate defenders and the rattle of musketfire echoed through the hills. Small artillery was rolled into position and began firing as well. There was no real coordination to any of the Union troops; they seemed to be acting independently, probing the Confederate line to gather information about their enemy's strength.

Hill, too, was confused about his enemy's intention and did not know where their main attack would take place. He rode to a lookout tower in Turner's Gap and was astonished by what he saw coming up the road. "The marching columns [of blue uniforms] extended back as far as the eye could see in the distance," he recalled. What he saw was an army of almost 28,000. "I do not remember ever to have experienced a feeling of greater loneliness."

There was little hope that his men, scattered as they were, could contain such an overwhelming force, and Hill anticipated a terrible beating. Then, stunningly, the endless line of blue came to a puzzling halt and did not move again for several hours. The delay gave Hill adequate time to gather enough troops to meet the onslaught that was sure to follow. He then sent an urgent request to Lee for support, or as he wrote later, "It was then I called so loudly for your help."

Reflecting the hesitancy of their commander, Union officers were moving very cautiously, unsure of the size of the enemy they might have to deal with in the tight confines of the mountain gaps. The commander in charge of the Union forces at Turner's Gap was General Ambrose Burnside, the man who had recently turned down Lincoln's offer to command the entire army.

Burnside decided that a straight-on attack up the National Road would be foolish, assuming that was where the rebels would concentrate most of their troops.

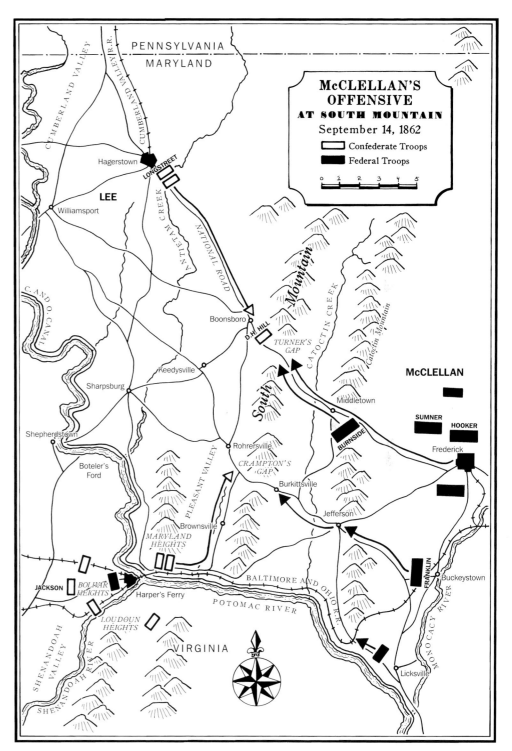

Instead, he called for a very complicated dual maneuver up two smaller gaps off the main road, hoping to get around both flanks of the Confederate line and drive all their forces out of the mountains. Getting his men into position took so much time that before Burnside was able to launch each attack, Lee had managed to get an additional 14,000 men there to reinforce Hill.

The two battles near Turner's Gap were intense, with charges and countercharges and dogged fighting by both sides. But the endless waves of Union soldiers finally began to push the beleaguered Confederate defenders back. "As they drew nearer," a Confederate gunner observed, "the whole country seemed to be full of bluecoats. They were so numerous that it looked as if they were creeping out of the ground."

Both Confederate flanks were slowly giving way, when the last of the reserve troops arrived to halt the complete collapse of the Confederate line. Another charge would have probably broken the Confederate troops, but darkness fell and the Union soldiers called it quits for the night.

While the fight at Turner's Gap was still in progress, Union forces numbering 12,000 approached a scrappy rebel force of 1,000 at Crampton's Gap. Confederate soldiers held the high ground there, well protected by stone walls and boulders. When the advancing Union soldiers attacked, they met fierce resistance that resulted in a two-hour battle that failed to dislodge the rebels.

After the first assault failed, the Union commander there, General William B. Franklin, worried that he was facing a superior force and spent several hours setting out his men for another attack. The preparations for battle were so extensive that one soldier quipped it was like a "lion making exceedingly careful preparations to spring on a plucky little mouse." This delay gave the Confederates time to bring in reinforcements.

Franklin eventually ordered his troops forward, and another savage encounter ensued. This time, the Union forces managed to outflank both sides of the enemy's line and drove them over the mountain in a panicked retreat. Then, to the complete astonishment of his own officers and soldiers, Franklin called a halt to any further advance, claiming he was outnumbered.

As the sun set and the fighting at Turner's Gap and Crampton's Gap lessened, the groans and cries of the wounded could be heard in the dark. Soldiers put down their weapons and began collecting their dead and wounded comrades. Losses to both sides that day were severe. The Union lost 2,325 wounded or killed, while the Confederate forces suffered 2,300 casualties.

Lee's men had managed, through luck and stubborn fighting, to halt the Union advance. But both Hill and another Confederate general, James Longstreet, knew that there was no way they could hold back Federal forces come daylight. They sent a message to Lee urging him to retreat.

Lee understood that his Maryland campaign was in danger. Two-thirds of his army was still engaged at Harper's Ferry, while his hold on South Mountain was tenuous at best. When his field generals reported that the enemy was poised to strike a killing blow, he relented. He decided to end his campaign and withdraw his army to Virginia. That night he sent out a courier with this melancholy message: "The day has gone against us and this army will go by Sharpsburg to cross the river."

*Searching by torchlight in the woods for wounded soldiers.*

# 6
# Retreat

**And tho' fortunes smiles be few,**
**Hope is always springing new,**
**Still inspiring me and you**
**With a magic, No Surrender!**
**—"No Surrender" by C. C. Mera, 1864**

A retreat is a complicated and dangerous procedure. The trick is to get tens of thousands of exhausted, dazed, and sometimes wounded soldiers away from the enemy as quickly and as quietly as possible. This is even more difficult at night in rugged and unfamiliar terrain.

Somewhere between ten and eleven that Sunday night, word was passed in whispers for Confederate soldiers to withdraw. Some ran off in haste, while others formed ragged lines and stumbled up the road toward Boonsboro. Major Moxley Sorrel remembered, "We had a bad night on the mountain" and that he and other officers often "had to play with the flats of our swords on the backs of . . . fellows" who refused to move quickly enough. Several men were so exhausted that they fell asleep before retreat was ordered and woke up the next morning, alone and surrounded by thousands of Federals.

Every road and lane leading toward Sharpsburg was jammed with Confederate soldiers. Countless men dropped from exhaustion and had to crawl to the side of the road or be trampled. To make matters worse, thirteen hundred Union horsemen led by Colonel Benjamin "Grimes" Davis were roaming through the countryside and striking at stragglers. Before sunrise on the fifteenth, Davis and his men came upon a two-mile-long line of Confederate supply wagons near Williamsport. The wagons were being driven by slaves and all of the Confederate guards were in the rear. Using the dark as cover, Davis rode to the front and used his best Southern accent to order the train up another road. Before the deception was discovered, Davis had captured half of the wagons.

Dawn also brought the Union army alive. Their advance pickets soon discovered that the rebel army had skedaddled during the night, and orders to pursue it were issued. McClellan hurriedly telegraphed Halleck with

*Drummer boy Private John White of Virginia found himself swept along toward Sharpsburg with the rest of the retreating Confederate army.*

the news, adding, "I am hurrying everything forward to endeavor to press their retreat to the utmost. The morale of our men is now restored." He then wired Ellen, "Have just learned that the enemy are retreating in a panic and that our victory is complete."

It certainly seemed that that was true, even to Lee. He had come to the North hoping to build on the numerous Confederate victories and persuade England and France to recognize and aid the Confederacy. Now his army and the dream of Southern independence hung in the balance.

McClellan had his main body of soldiers through South Mountain and marching toward Boonsboro. He also ordered William Franklin at Crampton's Gap to destroy the enemy in front of him. McClellan's message did nothing to inspire bold action. "It is important to drive in the enemy in your front," he told Franklin, "but be cautious in doing it until you have some idea of his force. . . . Thus far our success is complete, but let us follow it up closely, but warily."

Franklin had gotten reinforcements during the night, bringing his command to almost 20,000 men, well over twice the number of the enemy facing him. But he was paralyzed and failed to initiate a fight. When he heard cheering coming from the direction of Harper's Ferry, he assumed that the garrison had surrendered and sent McClellan a panicky note: "They outnumber me two to one," he told his commander. "It will of course not answer to pursue the enemy under these circumstances."

As his men watched impatiently from the heights of Crampton's Gap, the small rebel force that had so terrified Franklin quietly withdrew, ready to fight another day.

At about the same time, a courier found Lee and presented him with a message from Stonewall Jackson.

"Through God's blessing, Harper's Ferry and its garrison are to be surrendered." Several thousand soldiers would stay to guard the 13,000 prisoners and captured war materials, Jackson informed his commander, but "the other forces can move off this evening so soon as they get their rations."

Lee was near Sharpsburg when he read this and immediately came to a momentous decision. A line of ridges ran from the Potomac River to Antietam Creek, a distance of nearly four miles consisting of rocky outcroppings, woodlots, and rolling fields of corn. He saw in the terrain a perfect defensive position where his army could dig in against the enemy and save his campaign. He turned to his staff officers and told them, "We will make our stand on these hills."

Instantly new orders were written instructing field commanders to assemble their troops at Sharpsburg as quickly as possible.

While Lee was hastily putting men in line along Antietam Creek, McClellan entered Boonsboro to the rousing cheers of citizens and soldiers alike. "The welcome that he Received . . . must have done his heart good," wrote H. R. Dunham in his diary. "God bless General McClellan. Long may he lead. . . ."

The euphoria did not last long. By early afternoon a message arrived with ominous news. "A line of battle— or an arrangement of troops which looks very much like it—is formed on the other side of Antietam Creek and this side of Sharpsburg. It is four times longer on the west than on the east side of the road. . . ."

At this time, Lee had just 18,000 men with him at Sharpsburg. McClellan had nearly 55,000 at Boonsboro, with another 14,000 only six miles away. Yet McClellan launched no probing attacks and did not send cavalry across two undefended bridges and a number of fords to get an accurate estimate of Confederate strength. Instead, he spent the night moving men into position near Antietam Creek and waited for light.

On the sixteenth, he assembled a three-prong attack on the Confederate defenses, but never sent in more than

*Opposite page: A nervous-looking but heavily armed Union soldier stares into the lens of the camera.*

*Below: The moment they learned the rebel army was approaching, citizens of Sharpsburg gathered up as many of their belongings as possible and fled the town.*

20,000 men. Because McClellan failed to coordinate the attacks so they happened all at once, Lee was able to shift troops from one sector of the battlefield to another and halt each of the Federal advances.

Both sides settled in for the night, knowing that on the seventeenth a great battle would be fought. Years later, Union General Alpheus Williams remembered the evening vividly. "So dark, so obscure, so mysterious, so uncertain . . . there was a half-dreamy sensation about it all; but with a certain impression that the morrow was to be great with the future fate of our country. So much responsibility, so much intense, future anxiety!"

McClellan had promised Lincoln that he would destroy the enemy, but three times—at South Mountain on the fourteenth, on the morning of the fifteenth as the Confederate forces retreated, and again on the sixteenth—he failed to use the strength he had at his disposal and Lee slipped from his grasp.

Now the enemy waited, their backs to the Potomac, daring him to attack. Little Mac also sensed that, back

*Union soldiers stretch out for a night's sleep near a line of cannons.*

in Washington, Abraham Lincoln and Henry Halleck waited at the War Department, willing him to attack in force.

There would be a battle in the morning, he knew. A big one. McClellan was prone to grand pronouncements, but he made one that night that was also prophetic: "We are through for the night," he announced to his staff, "but tomorrow we fight the battle that will determine the fate of the Republic."

# ✷ 7 ✷
# A Great Tumbling Together

I hear the sounds of the different missiles, the short *t-h-t! t-h-t!* of the rifle balls,
I see the shells exploding leaving small white clouds, I hear great shells shrieking as they pass,
The grape like the hum and whirr of wind through the trees, (tumultuous now the contest rages.)
—"The Artilleryman's Vision" by Walt Whitman, 1865

The first vague glimmers of light appeared at around 5:15 on September 17. Slowly, the outlines of the battlefield emerged, softened by wisps of clinging fog. Union General Joe Hooker rode his horse up to an advance picket line and inspected the terrain in front of his men.

McClellan had given Hooker the tough assignment of attacking the enemy's left wing. Once he had engaged the enemy, Union forces under other generals were then going to attack the Confederate right wing and center as well. McClellan's hope was that Lee would respond to Hooker's advance by withdrawing soldiers from these other positions, making them more vulnerable to the following attacks.

Hooker's objective was a mile away and easily seen—an open plateau east of the turnpike that was filled with Confederate cannons. His plan was to launch the majority of his 8,600 infantrymen down the turnpike toward the church of the German Baptist Brethren (known as the Dunkers because of their baptism by total immersion in water) and seize the woods behind it. Another smaller force in the East Woods would attack along the Smoketown Road.

The Confederate forces in this section of the battlefield were under the command of General Stonewall Jackson. Jackson, who looked like an avenging Old Testament prophet, drove his officers and men unsparingly and had an uncanny instinct for victory. "His name was a terror in the Union army," a soldier from Massachusetts confessed, "and with us expressed more fear than all the other names put together." Stonewall had only 7,700 men, but he had a strong defensive position on high ground and the iron will to hold it.

Shortly after Hooker's reconnaissance the Union opened a 100-cannon barrage, which the Confederates immediately answered. The massive booming echoed like distant thunder, shaking the ground. Gray, acrid smoke rolled and drifted to obscure the West Woods and

*Union General Joseph Hooker was in charge of the first attack on the left side of the Confederate battle line.*

*A very determined-looking General Stonewall Jackson was in charge of defending the left side of the Confederate battle line. He would meet every charge by Hooker's men with one of his own.*

nearby turnpike. McClellan's big 20-pounder Parrot guns joined the duel, sending shells screaming two miles through the air to rip up cornfields and vegetable gardens.

In the middle of this deafening cannon duel, gunners noticed something unusual just above a grassy field. The door to the Nicodemus farmhouse was suddenly flung open and a number of terrified women and children sprinted out. They looked "like a flock of birds," recalled rebel Captain William Blackford, "hair streaming in the wind and children of all ages stretched out behind."

The group headed for the safety of the Confederate lines, but their flight became bogged down in the deep, loose soil of a recently plowed field. "Every time one would fall," Captain Blackford went on, "the rest thought it was the result of a cannon shot and ran faster."

Blackford thought the scene humorous at first, but then remembered his sense of chivalry and galloped across the field. He swung several children up behind him, then calmly led the rest of the group to safety. He was pleased to note that the Yankee guns fell silent during the ten minutes it took to rescue the group. After the brief lull, the cannon fire resumed.

Drowned out by the roar of the big guns was the sharp sound of musketfire as both sides sniped at each other. In preparation for the planned charge, Federal troops in the East Woods laid down one deadly volley

after another to cut up the small force of rebels at the Mumma farm. The Confederate troops were pulling back, when the Union soldiers began to run out of ammunition. As they withdrew to allow fresh troops to replace them, another Union officer nearby mistook them in the dense smoke for Confederate troops and thought he was about to be overrun. He called for his men to retreat and the fighting in this section slacked off momentarily.

As this was taking place, another Union attack force moved into position at the northern edge of what would come to be called the Cornfield. At 6 a.m. Union artillery there switched from exploding shells to canisters and fired several rounds into the head-high corn. Each canister had a fuse that would explode it to send thousands of metal pellets into the face of the enemy. After several rounds were fired, a brigade of 1,100 Union soldiers plunged into the corn.

At the southern end of the Cornfield, the rebel infantrymen waited patiently behind piles of fence rails, their guns pointed directly at the corn in front of them. When Union men finally emerged, the Confederate soldiers "poured into us a terrible fire," as Union soldier Henry Shaefer remembered.

The volley dropped scores of bluecoats and stunned the survivors enough that their charge shuddered and paused. Then more Union men came forward, stepping over the wounded and dead, all the while firing at the enemy. In earlier battles, when most of the men were new to fighting, such intense firing might prompt large numbers of them to run for their lives. But they were veterans now and used to the noise and screams and not about to be frightened off. The next moment, the rebel line rose up to face their enemy, and for several desperate minutes both

*While shells explode and men are shot around them, Union troops
march in formation past the Dunker Church.*

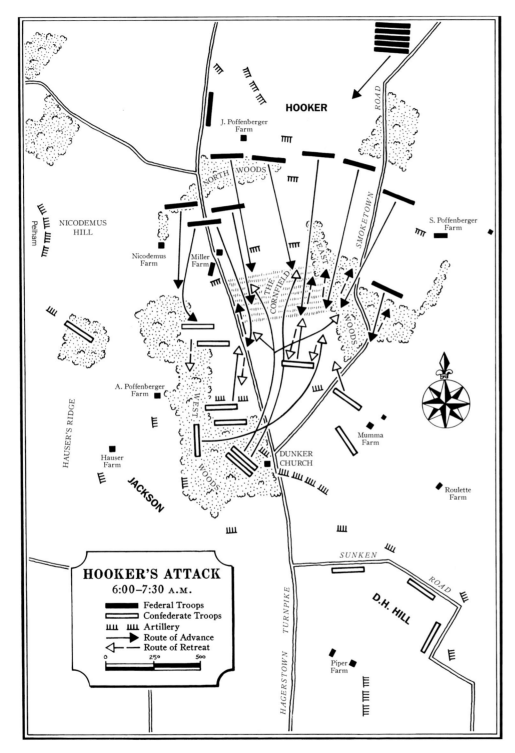

**HOOKER'S ATTACK**
6:00–7:30 A.M.

▬▬ Federal Troops
▭▭ Confederate Troops
⊥⊥⊥ Artillery
➤ Route of Advance
◁— Route of Retreat

0      250      500

sides stood in plain sight of each other, loading and firing as quickly as possible.

The shouted orders of officers and the screams of the wounded went unheard as the killing frenzy intensified. A small group of rebel reinforcements arrived to help their comrades, just as additional Yankee forces attacked from the side. Both sides, at last exhausted and stunned, finally lay down behind whatever cover they could find and continued to fight.

The Union troops were running low on ammunition and when no reinforcements came forward to replace them, the officer in charge ordered his men to pull back through the Cornfield. Seeing the enemy retreating, a rebel officer shouted for his men to advance and was shocked when only a few responded. When he investigated, he discovered sixty of his men on the ground behind a ledge, every one of them dead.

Two Union brigades had indeed been assigned to reinforce the charge of the lead brigade, but their command structure had disintegrated. One general had been severely wounded while reconnoitering, while the other fled his men and the battlefield with what his men called "cowardly legs." After many minutes of confusion, one of the brigades plunged through the Cornfield only to be met by the blaze of a hundred rebel muskets firing all at once.

"Just in front of us a house was burning," wrote a New York soldier, "and the fire and smoke, flashing of muskets and whizzing of bullets, yells of men, etc., were perfectly horrible."

Johnathan Stowe had just stepped out of the corn when his right leg was nearly torn off by a flying piece of hot metal. Unable to move, with cannonshot and minie bullets whirring overhead, he pulled out his pocket diary and pencil. "Battle Oh horrid battle," he managed to scrawl. "What sights I have seen. I am wounded! And am afraid shall be again as shells fly past me every few seconds carrying away limbs from the trees. . . . Am in severe pain. How the shells fly. I do sincerely hope shall not be wounded again."

Like Stowe, thousands of other men would be wounded and stranded on the field of battle, hoping to survive until rescued. Of the 1,100 men in the first brigade through the Cornfield, over one third of them were either killed or wounded. The second brigade across had suffered 224 casualties out of 334 men.

By this time, survivors on both sides were scrambling among the dead and wounded, searching for cartridges. More rebel reinforcements stormed the Cornfield, while their artillery poured round after round into the East Woods. Finally, the last Union brigade sorted out its command and entered the field, halting the most recent Confederate advance. By 7 a.m. the two sides had inflicted incredible damage on each other and had come to a kind of sputtering stalemate.

At about this time, the main Union attack force began marching down the Hagerstown Turnpike in two long columns. No sooner had they begun moving than a shell exploded in the middle of the road, killing two and wounding eleven. More shells rained in as Confederate artillery on the hills found their range.

A great deal of this cannonfire was coming from Nicodemus Hill, two thousand feet away. Although the cannons were out in the open, no Union officer ever bothered to mount a charge against these guns during the entire battle. The only attempt to silence them came from artillery batteries over a mile away, and these were not very effective.

*Twenty-year-old Confederate Private Thomas Taylor was just south of the Cornfield when he was severely wounded in the knee. He would lie on the battlefield all day and all night and would be crippled for the rest of his life.*

Their ranks thinned but undaunted, the Union regiment pushed on. As they neared the Miller farm they entered a thick patch of morning fog and battle smoke. Suddenly, Confederate skirmishers in the Miller pasture opened fire on the men as they walked past, and then, a moment later, hundreds of rebels popped up from a clover field and sent a surprise volley into the Union ranks.

"Men, I can not say fell," remembered Major Rufus Dawes, "they were knocked out of the ranks by the dozens." Dawes's men returned fire, screaming angrily

560

as they struggled to load. "Men and officers of New York and Wisconsin are fused into a common mass, in a frantic struggle to shoot fast. Everybody tears cartridges, loads, passes guns, or shoots. Men are falling in their places or running back into the [nearby] corn."

One sixteen-year-old Union soldier was struck by a bullet in the left side of the neck and toppled to the ground. Mary Galloway had put on a uniform and joined the army just a few days before to search for her boyfriend, but found a bullet instead. She rolled into a shallow ravine, bleeding and in excruciating pain, unable to move as the battle went on around her.

Union skirmishers moved into the clover field to drive the rebels back, and the march continued with one column veering off to enter the Cornfield. Just as this was happening, 1,150 rebels came pouring out of the West Woods and made it all the way to a fence that ran along the west side of the turnpike. There they sent heavy fire into the Federals who were in a pasture not more than one hundred feet away.

These new Confederate forces found themselves being shot at by soldiers in the pasture, in the Cornfield, and near the West Woods behind them, plus artillery from the Miller barnyard. This Confederate counter-charge managed to halt the Union advance, but at a ghastly cost in lives.

When their commander was mortally wounded, they were ordered to pull back. A lieutenant from Virginia, Richard Jennings, was wounded in the hip by an exploding shell and announced that, "I am going out of here." A wounded soldier next to him told him it would be better to lie down than try to outrun the enemy bullets. "I may as well be killed running as lying still," he told his comrade as he got to his feet. "I just

let out and ran like a deer," he recalled, "and made it to the timber, but I was almost scared to death when I got there."

The Federal advance began moving again and seemed unstoppable. A rebel officer made his way to a group of reserves bivouacked behind the Dunker church. In a controlled, formal voice, this officer presented himself to Brigadier General John Bell Hood. "General Lawton sends his compliments with the request that you come at once to his support," he announced, adding that General Lawton had been wounded.

Hood had been waiting impatiently for this request since the shelling had begun. Minutes later his 2,300 men came rushing out of the woods to cross the turnpike in front of the church, screaming the rebel yell as they did. They then unleashed a ferocious volley that stopped the Union advance in its tracks.

A Union officer complained that, "We were almost as good a target as a barn. It is terrible to march slowly into danger, and see and feel each second your chance of death is surer than it was the second before."

Somehow, Major Dawes survived this volley, though it was "like a scythe running through our line." When their color-bearer was shot down, Dawes picked up the flag and waved it over his head to rally his men. "When I took that color in my hand, I gave up all hope of life," he would write. "It did not occur to me as possible that I could carry that flag into the deadly storm and live [since] (four men had fallen under it)."

While the Federal forces were regrouping, Hood hurried his men into a battle line that stretched from the turnpike to the East Woods. He then began advancing them. Years later, he still remembered having to guide his horse very carefully around the dead and wounded.

*Alexander Gardner took this photograph of Confederate dead along the Hagerstown Pike one day after the battle ended.*

*Long columns
of Union soldiers
come up and over
a hill to attack
Confederate forces.*

Another Union counterattack was launched, this time supported by artillery firing into the rebel line. The two sides were so close that the shells were set to explode just one and a half seconds after leaving the muzzles. A Union officer saw a shell explode and "an arm go 30 feet into the air and fall back again. . . . It was just awful."

"Whole ranks went down," Brigadier General John Gibbon recalled, "and after we got possession of the field, dead men were found piled on top of one another."

There was now fierce fighting in every section of this portion of the battlefield. Some of it was well-coordinated with ordered lines, organized assaults, and quick, calm exchanges of fresh troops for exhausted ones. In other places, the fighting was haphazard and without discipline, men loading and firing with such frenzy that they sometimes shot into their own ranks.

In the thick smoke, troops moved about, searching for the enemy. A group of Ohio soldiers stumbled upon another from Pennsylvania at the edge of the Cornfield, mistook them for rebels, and delivered a killing volley of fire directly into their flank. "The sight at the fence," Colonel Eugene Powell wrote, "where [they were] standing when we gave our first fire, was awful beyond description. . . . Dead men were literally piled upon and across each other. . . ."

These Federal forces charged into the Cornfield and savage hand-to-hand combat followed. Men were stabbed with bayonets or clubbed with musket barrels. For several frantic minutes the fighting went on, but the Confederate soldiers were finally beginning to withdraw.

Private Benjamin Witcher from Georgia glanced around and saw rows of butternut-clad troops lying in formation and decided to fight with them. When he tried to get another man to stay, his friend screamed that the men on the ground were all dead. Witcher yelled back that they were not. His friend then fired his weapon into the back of one of the men and when the body didn't even twitch, Witcher retreated with the rest of his comrades.

The Confederate retreat would be halted in time to hold the West Woods, but Union forces were able to seize the Dunker church and establish a position on the plateau.

Robert E. Lee watched all of this swirling action from a grove of trees near his headquarters in Sharpsburg. He was outnumbered and knew that if McClellan committed enough troops to attack his left flank or launched attacks on his center and right flank simultaneously, he would be routed and driven from the field. Reinforcements had begun arriving from Harper's Ferry, but they needed to be rested before being sent into action. Even though he risked exposing his right flank, he ordered several thousand men shifted to strengthen his weakening left and hoped that McClellan would be as timid as always.

McClellan, meanwhile, had his headquarters at the large brick home of Philip Pry, some two miles from the action. Easy chairs were brought from the parlor, and telescopes were mounted on stakes to view the unfolding battle.

One of his aides, Colonel David Strother, was impressed by McClellan's calm demeanor, sitting in his easy chair, smoking a cigar and chatting with his second in command, Major General Fitz John Porter. "[Porter's] observations he communicated to the commander by nods, signs, or in words so low-toned and brief that the nearest by-standers had but little benefit with them." At one point a communication was received by flag-signal, and McClellan was heard to say, "All goes well; Hooker is driving them."

The truth, of course, was somewhat different. While Union troops now held the Dunker church and had artillery on the plateau, the rebel forces hadn't broken. They still maintained strong defensive positions on Nicodemus Hill and in the West Woods and reinforcements were being filed in. What is more, so many Federal officers had been wounded or killed that the Union forces were temporarily rudderless.

Brigadier General Alpheus Williams sent a message by flag to McClellan's headquarters. "Genl. Mansfield is dangerously wounded. Genl. Hooker wounded severely in foot. Genl. Sumner I hear is advancing. We hold the field at present. Please give us all the aid you can. . . ."

There is no record of what McClellan said to this urgent request, but we do know what his thinking was. He still labored under the belief that Robert E. Lee's forces outnumbered him and that somehow Lee was setting up some sort of elaborate trap. So McClellan did not send in reinforcements to complete the assault on the Confederate left wing. Nor did he launch any other attacks immediately. He chose instead to do nothing.

A lull settled over the battlefield broken by sporadic sniper fire and the occasional rumble of cannons. On both sides those lucky enough to be uninjured went to find wounded friends and drag them to safety. A Wisconsin soldier who had battled and survived the Cornfield described the fighting as "a great tumbling together of all heaven and earth—the slaughter on both sides was enormous."

He had no idea how accurate he was. In the opening hours of the battle, 27,000 men had faced each other for possession of approximately 160 acres of land. Of these, 8,700 of them were either dead or wounded by nine o'clock. And there was still plenty of daylight left to carry on the fight.

*Nineteen-year-old Union Private Harrison White was a first cousin of General McClellan. He was shot somewhere near Dunker Church and taken to a makeshift hospital on the Hoffman farm, where he died that night.*

General Edwin "Bull" Sumner was commander of the second major attack on the Confederate lines.

# ⋆ 8 ⋆
# The Sunken Road

March onward, soldiers, onward; the strife is begun;
Loud bellowing rolls the boom of the black-throated gun;
The rifles are cracking, the torn banners toss,
The sabers are clashing, the bayonets cross.
—"Trumpet Song" by Oliver Wendell Holmes Sr., 1889

Major General Edwin Vose Sumner of the Union army was angry as he listened to the fighting for Dunker church. He believed that the best way to crush the Confederate left flank would have been to have his 15,200 soldiers strike at the same time as Hooker's did and not "sending these troops into that action in driblets." But McClellan delayed Sumner's attack because of his belief that thousands of hidden rebel soldiers were waiting somewhere to surprise him.

Now at long last the order arrived and Sumner was leading his men toward the battle. From headquarters an observer watched these new troops heading into the fight and wrote, "With flags flying and the long unfaltering lines rising and falling as they crossed the rolling fields, it looked as though nothing could stop them."

When they reached the East Woods at nine o'clock, the terrible sounds of the morning's battle had dimmed to the occasional crack of a musket and the heart-wrenching screams of the wounded. "Not an enemy appeared," General Alpheus Williams would report. "The woods in front were as quiet as any sylvan shade could be."

The lull was deceptive. While McClellan fretted about phantom enemy soldiers and effectively stalled the Federal advance, Robert E. Lee was hurriedly repositioning thousands of men and hoping they would be in place in time to meet this new challenge.

Lee had been helped to mount his horse and was able to personally supervise the strengthening of one vital position. This was a deeply etched road that ran the entire width of the valley, zigzagging from the Hagerstown turnpike to the Boonsboro turnpike. Called Sunken Road, it had been eaten away by generations of farmers' wagons until it was several feet below ground level in places and made a natural trench from which soldiers could fire on the enemy. An hour before, only a few hundred Confederate soldiers had been positioned in

*He may look like a mere boy, but twenty-four-year-old Major John Pelham directed Confederate artillery fire with deadly accuracy.*

Sunken Road. Now, as Sumner's men drew closer, more than 2,600 Confederates were settled into this natural shooting gallery, their fingers on the triggers of their weapons.

Sumner reached the East Woods with the lead brigade and began preparing his men for an immediate charge. Alpheus Williams had been on the battlefield since sunrise and came forward to brief Sumner on enemy positions. Sumner brushed him off, impatient to put his men into the fight.

Sumner's nickname was "Bull," because he had a booming voice that could be heard in the middle of the loudest cannon barrage. Behind his back he was called "Bull Head," a not very complimentary name he'd

earned when an enemy bullet allegedly bounced off his thick skull. He was tough and brave and stubborn and he decided that the quiet battlefield was an indication that the enemy was fought out and vulnerable.

Without reconnoitering enemy positions or searching for the best places to strike, Sumner formed the 7,500 men of the lead brigade into three neat columns and proceeded to march them west directly across the Cornfield. He intended to cross the turnpike and advance to the West Woods where his column would turn left to form a strong battle line. From this position they could then sweep the woods clean of the enemy and control that side of the battlefield.

The weakness of this procedure was obvious. The columns were only fifty yards apart, so close together that enemy fire could easily rip them apart if it came from the correct angle. What is more, Sumner had set out without notifying the trailing brigade of Brigadier General William French where he was going. French's brigade would ordinarily follow behind the lead brigade to give it support and counter any surprise moves by the enemy. Instead, when French later arrived on the scene and found Sumner gone, he took his men south toward the Mumma farmstead.

All of this was seen at headquarters and a warning was sent: "General McClellan desires you to be very careful how you advance, as he fears our right is suffering." Bull Sumner was riding with this lead group and never received the message.

The opening minutes of the advance went without incident. The biggest obstacle the men faced was stepping over the dead and wounded lying amid the bent cornstalks. At one point a colonel from Michigan stopped to chat with a wounded rebel. "You fought and stood well," he told the young man. "Yes," came the sullen reply, "and here we lie."

Everything went according to plan until the Union soldiers reached the turnpike. Just as the lead soldiers began climbing through what was left of the rail fence, Confederate shells began raining down on them. Bodies mixed with great clots of earth and were blown into the air as huge gaps were punched in the Union line. Confederate Major John Pelham had seen the advancing Federals and moved his horse-drawn artillery from Nicodemus Hill to a high ridge behind the Hauser farmhouse. From here he could easily lob shots into the neat blue columns coming toward him.

Bull Sumner and his officers raced back and forth urging the men to tighten up their ranks and push forward. With heads bowed, his troops struggled on even though their close formation was a clear problem. "The projectile that went over the heads of the first line," noted Lieutenant Colonel Francis Palfrey, "was likely to find its billet in the second or third."

Despite heavy losses and continued shelling, Union troops made it across the turnpike and into the woods north of the Dunker church. A few minutes later they left the shelter of these trees and found themselves in an open field. Immediately, John Pelham swung his cannons around and fired into the Federalists at close range, while several hundred rebel skirmishers began picking away at their ranks.

At the same time, a group of approximately eight hundred Union soldiers composed mostly of raw recruits from Pennsylvania crossed the turnpike and veered left to head toward the Dunker church. They were halted a few hundred yards short of the building when they came under heavy enemy sniper fire.

After a few minutes of spirited volleying, the officer

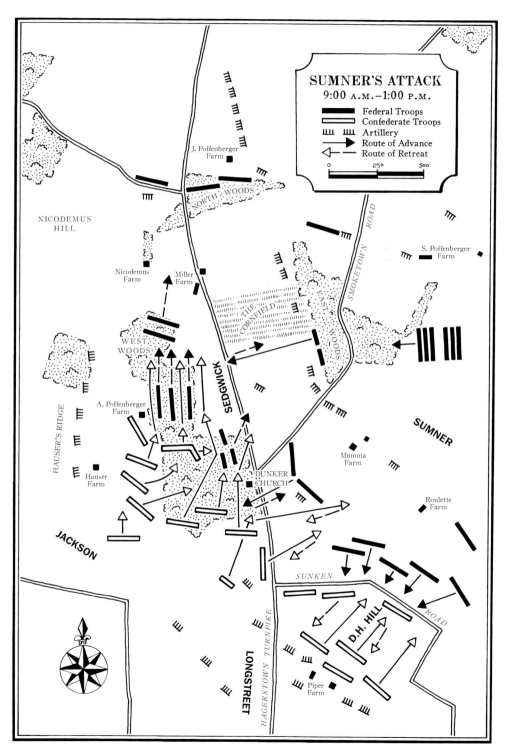

Skirmish between the Brooklyn 14th and 300 Rebel Cavalry

*Close-quarter fighting in the woods behind the Dunker Church.*

in charge of the Pennsylvania troops began to grow nervous. His men had performed well so far, but they were running low on ammunition and needed support if he hoped to hold his position much longer. He gave his horse to an aide and told him to hurry back to request reinforcements. The aide had barely ridden away when the woods around the Pennsylvania troops came alive with shouts and gunfire as hundreds of butternut uniforms surged forward.

Meanwhile, in the open field beyond the West Woods, additional Confederate infantry attacked Bull Sumner's lead brigade of Union soldiers. They poured three successive volleys into the exposed side of the Union line, which was frantically attempting to maneuver to counter this assault.

Sumner was at the very front of this brigade when the attack was launched and immediately understood the danger his men were in. "By God, we must get out of this!" he screamed, galloping off toward the rear to alert the men there.

He had barely reached the trailing soldiers when a swarm of Confederates came up to attack the rear. "We were completely flanked on the left," a startled Jonathan Peacock recalled, "and in two minutes more could have been prisoners of war if Gen Sumner himself had not road in through a terrific fire of the enemy and brought us off. . . . My men fell around me like dead flies on a frosty morning."

More Confederate troops joined the three-sided assault and the Yankees began to withdraw north. Some maintained a sense of order and even stopped now and again to shoot at the enemy. Others ran in a wild panic.

While retreating, Captain Oliver Wendell Holmes Jr. was hit in the neck and fell in a heap. He was drifting in and out of consciousness when the regimental chaplain bent over him. "You're a Christian, aren't you?" the nervous chaplain asked. Holmes was unable to speak, but he managed to nod his head. "Well then, that's all right!" the chaplain responded, and then ran off to save his own skin.

The Union forces fled through the Miller's meadow, past the Nicodemus farmhouse, and did not stop running until they reached the protection of the North Woods. The Confederate forces pressed their advantage hard, trailing after the retreating Federals.

A wounded Union soldier, Norwood P. Hollowell, was huddling in the Nicodemus house with scores of other casualties when the Southerners swept past. One rebel popped his head in a window and was surprised to see so many wounded soldiers lying there, begging for water. He tossed in his canteen and sprinted off to rejoin the fight.

As the canteen was passed around, Hollowell heard the thudding boom of artillery to the north as Union batteries targeted the Confederate troops. "In about fifteen minutes that good-hearted fellow came back to the window all out of breath, saying, 'Hurry up there! Hand me my canteen! I am on the double-quick myself now!'"

The cannonfire had temporarily halted the Confederate charge and sent them scurrying back to the West Woods. The battle then shifted slightly south to focus on the Sunken Road.

While Sumner was marching his men into a doomed charge, General French was taking his 5,700 men south past the Mumma farm and across the fields of William Roulette. He had decided on his own to support the Pennsylvania troops that were under attack at the Dunker church by seizing the land beyond the Sunken Road.

Facing this wave of blue were the 2,600 Confederate soldiers lying on the inside bank of the road, their rifles resting on rails and ready. Lee, his hands still in splints, and the field commander of these troops, General D. H. Hill, had watched French's endless line of soldiers advancing and must have looked concerned. A colonel from Alabama, John B. Gordon, saw the two men and called out reassuringly, "The men are going to stay here, General, till the sun goes down or victory is won!" Before long, it would seem to Gordon that the sun might never set.

After clearing the Roulette farm of enemy snipers, French's troops found themselves in open fields that angled up to the Sunken Road. Even though they made perfect targets for the waiting rebels, no shots were fired and French's men came on. When they were one hundred yards from the rail fences, they were ordered to fix bayonets in anticipation of a charge.

The Confederate troops in the Sunken Road had been ordered to hold their fire until the enemy got to a ridge some eighty yards away. With the quiet patience of hunters in a giant duck blind, D. H. Hill's men took steady aim.

When the lead Federal line crested the ridge, the Confederates unleashed a thunderous volley that, as Colonel F. M. Parker would recall, "brought down the enemy as grain falls before a reaper." Soldiers standing behind those shooting, loaded weapons and passed them forward to keep a deadly stream of fire pouring in. Colonel Gordon was by nature a tough warhorse, but even he was stunned by what this volleying did to the enemy. "The effect was appalling. The entire front line, with few exceptions, went down in the consuming blast."

In the opening five minutes of this clash, over 450 Federals were killed or wounded. The "few exceptions" still able to move fell back beyond the ridge and pressed themselves as close to the ground as possible. The second brigade of Union soldiers soon came up behind the remains of the lead brigade and began firing into the clouds of billowing musket smoke. These "troops didn't know what they were expected to do," a frustrated Captain Samuel Fiske explained, "and sometimes, in their excitement, fired at their own men."

The survivors of the lead brigade now found themselves being shot at from the front and rear. The very next moment, they were running back to the Mumma farm, "crying," Captain Fiske said, "'skedaddle, skedaddle!'" as they did. He went on to explain that, "Some of our men tried to stop them; and a few of them, it must be confessed, joined in their flight."

Those who did not flee tried to continue the advance with some of Fiske's "men firing with precision and deliberation, though some shut their eyes, and fired up in the air." Such haphazard musketry did nothing to slacken the rebel volleys. Added to them was the thudding boom of shells exploding all around. One shell plowed through a row of Mr. Roulette's beehives and sent an angry swarm of bees into the Union lines.

A brief Confederate countercharge was stopped by accurate Union cannon fire, followed by another Union charge led by Brigadier General Nathan Kimball. "Now boys, we are going, and we'll stay with them all day if they want us to!" screamed Kimball to his soldiers.

The line staggered on and was immediately blasted by volley after volley. A sixteen-year-old Union soldier

1864.

*Left: Thomas Galwey joined the Union army in 1861, when he was fifteen years old.*

◆

*Opposite page: In order to remove places where enemy snipers could hide, Union troops burned the home and barn of Samuel Mum and other Sharpsburg farmers.*

from Wisconsin, Thomas Galwey, was in the middle of the slaughter. In previous battles, the teenager remembered, "our fighting had been mostly of the desultory, skirmishing sort. What we see now looks to us like systematic killing." The survivors began pulling back and Galwey heard General Kimball muttering, "God save my poor boys!"

Another brigade of Union soldiers came charging up the hill, only to be hit by a concentration of heavy fire from the Sunken Road. More Confederate reserves appeared and began firing from the field behind the road, causing yet another Union retreat.

A reporter for the *New York Tribune*, Albert Richardson, took in the scene of battle and wrote, "On the great field were riderless horses and scattering men, clouds of dirt from solid shot and exploding shells, long dark lines of infantry swaying to and fro, with columns of smoke rising from their muskets, red flashes and white puffs from the batteries—with the sun shining brightly on all this scene of tumult." The noise of the fighting was overwhelming, Richardson would report, "a savage continual thunder that cannot compare to any sound I ever heard."

When Union artillery targeted the troops stationed behind Sunken Road, the men there rushed forward to the safety of the road. The crush of men in the road was so overwhelming that an officer called for a charge and hundreds of Confederate soldiers streamed over the rail fence only to be cut down by the enemy.

Another Union charge was launched and this time a Union colonel was relieved that "The shouts of our men, and their sudden dash toward the sunken road, so startled the enemy that their fire visibly slackened, their line wavered, and squads of two and three began leaving the road and running into the corn [behind them]."

A soldier from Georgia saw the stampede begin. "The slaughter was terrible!" he would write later in his diary. "When ordered to retreat I could scarcely extricate myself from the dead and wounded around me."

Sergeant James Shinn withdrew with the rest of his North Carolina comrades. "The minnie balls, shot & shell rained upon us. . . . Many officers were killed & wounded [and many] I am sorry & ashamed to say, left the field unhurt."

Watching the action from the Pry house was another journalist, Charles Coffin. "Up the slope moves the line to the top of the knoll," he would tell the readers of the *Boston Journal*. "Ah! What a crash! A white cloud, gleams of lightning, a yell, a hurrah, and then up in the corn-field a great commotion, men firing into each other's faces, the Confederate line breaking, the ground strewn with prostrate forms."

McClellan watched all this with growing excitement and at one point blurted out, "It is the most beautiful field I ever saw, and the grandest battle!"

Despite his pleasure with the developments on the field, McClellan still feared the unseen enemy. When more artillery support was requested from his generals in battle, he sent forward only one of three hundred reserve batteries available. He did agree to commit several additional brigades to the fight, but he had positioned them so far away that it would take nearly two hours for them to arrive on the scene. Proper support would have probably headed off what was about to happen.

As Union soldiers crossed the Sunken Road and entered the cornfield behind it, they heard a stupendous explosion and a wave of rapid musketfire from the direction of the Dunker church. This was the massive rebel

*Twenty-eight-year-old Confederate Dr. William S. Parran was near the Sunken Road when several men firing artillery were injured. He immediately volunteered to man the gun, only to be shot dead a few minutes later.*

counterattack that had been set in motion against the new recruits from Pennsylvania.

The screaming Confederates seemed to come at the recruits from every direction. The Pennsylvania troops received the first volley bravely, but when a second and third poured in, they broke and ran back across the Hagerstown Turnpike. "You could hear laughing, cursing, yelling and the groans of the wounded and dying, while the awful roar of the musketry was appalling," Sergeant William Andrews told his family back in Georgia. "Where the [Union] line stood the ground was covered in blue, and I believe I could have walked on them without putting my feet on the ground."

Eager to press their advantage, some of the Confederates surged after the Federals and were able to capture one of the Yankee guns in the chaos. "[Our] men came scampering to the rear in great confusion," Union General Williams said later. "The Rebels followed with a yell but three or four of our batteries being in position they were received with a tornado of canister. . . . They fell in the very front of the line and all along it apparently, stirring up a dust like a thick cloud. When the dust blew away no regiment and not a living [enemy] was to be seen."

In the meanwhile, retreating Confederates from the Sunken Road had stopped and regrouped and held the advancing Federals in place in the cornfield. "At this point Genl. D. H. Hill was with us in person walking up and down our lines and speaking words of encouragement," Major Moxley Sorrel would recount. Then "Genl. Hill in a clear loud voice gave the order—*Attention—Charge!*"

Rebels advanced on the run, shooting as they did, while Union soldiers stood in Sunken Road to return the fire. Colonel Edward Cross evidently became infuriated by the rebel yell he was hearing and screamed at his men, "Put on the war paint! Give'em the war whoop!" His men smeared their faces with black powder ripped from cartridges and commenced to howl as loud as they could. His reanimated men stood their ground and eventually the rebel charge was driven back.

While the battle raged, a civilian wagon filled with medical supplies came rumbling down the Smoketown Road and turned in at Sam Poffenberger's farm. The driver was a forty-year-old clerk in the U.S. Patent Office, but today Clara Barton was at Antietam to minister to the injured and dying. Already dozens of wounded soldiers had been brought to Poffenberger's yard and Clara immediately began dressing their wounds. At one point, a stray bullet tore a gaping hole in the sleeve of her blouse and killed a man as she was giving him water. Clara Barton would remain on the battlefield for three straight days and did not leave until her wagon was completely empty.

Back at McClellan's a member of the headquarter guard watched with horrified fascination as the battle unfolded before him. "We are having a terrible battle," Eugene Carter would write home to his folks. "It commenced at daylight this morning and has been raging furiously all day. All other battles in this country are merely skirmishes compared to it."

The Battle of Antietam was only seven hours old at the time and already the fields, pastures, orchards, and barnyards were strewn with over 18,500 dead or wounded Union and Confederate soldiers. This was when the Union attack on the Confederate right flank commenced.

*While many historians would describe the outcome of
the Battle of Antietam as a draw, this Currier and Ives
illustration implies that the Confederate troops were routed.*

# ✹ 9 ✹
# Burnside's Bridge

The flags of war like storm-birds fly,
The charging trumpets blow,
Yet rolls no thunder in the sky,
No earthquake strives below.

And, calm and patient, Nature keeps
Her ancient promise well,
Though o'er her bloom and greenness sweeps
The battle's breath of hell.

—"The Battle Autumn of 1862" by John Greenleaf Whittier, 1862

*The final assault on the Confederate line was commanded by General Ambrose E. Burnside.*

The third and last part of the Confederate battle line to come under attack was its right flank. Union General Ambrose E. Burnside had over 13,000 men under his command, plus McClellan's explicit promise to reinforce him with an additional 10,000 if Burnside requested aid. Against them, Lee could muster only 4,000 soldiers, most of the others having been moved to reinforce the center and left flanks. While vastly outnumbered, the Confederate troops had strong defensive positions, tucked in on high ground thick with trees and boulders.

McClellan's plan called for a charge across the Rohrbach Bridge to establish a Union force on the Confederate side of Antietam Creek. McClellan assumed this would compel Lee to hold troops there to counter the charge, which would mean Lee couldn't reassign any of that force to help out in other parts of the battlefield.

The plan was perfectly sound, except that McClellan did not order Burnside to attack until 9:30, well after the fighting to the north had begun. Compounding the delay, Burnside was slow to organize and launch his men. Several days before, McClellan had chastised Burnside for allowing the Confederate troops in South Mountain to slip away so easily and removed part of his command. The ordinarily cheerful and obliging Burnside might very well have been sulking over this slight, and was slow to

place, three hundred other soldiers from Ohio were to storm the bridge in a headlong rush. The third and main force—some 3,200 strong—was to cross the creek at a ford almost three-quarters of a mile south of the bridge. Once across they were to strike at the Confederate troops from the side.

The Connecticut troops under Colonel Henry Kingsbury made it to the creek in good order and established a skirmish line along the banks. Confederate sharpshooters hidden in the leafy trees across the way were soon picking off Kingsbury's men with ease. When a group of Union soldiers attempted to cross the thirty-yards-wide stream, a Georgia infantry unit opened fire, systematically shooting down the soldiers floundering in the water, including the captain leading them. A second attempt to ford the creek was stopped when Kingsbury was hit four times and the Union troops withdrew, carrying Kingsbury to a nearby farmhouse where he later died.

As planned, the Ohio troops under Colonel George Crook charged when they heard fighting below the bridge. Crook, however, had failed to study the terrain and had forgotten to bring along a local guide. He led his men into a dense woods, became confused and wandered about for nearly a half hour, emerging at a place on the creek almost 1,000 feet above the bridge. He and his men took cover and spent the rest of the day shooting at Confederates across the water and were of no real value to taking the bridge.

While all this was occurring, the main attack force under the command of Brigadier General Isaac Rodman arrived at the ford they were to use. The location had been picked by young army engineers who clearly didn't know their business. The banks were very steep, with the one on the Union side rising up nearly 160 feet. Besides

respond to anything McClellan ordered. By the time his forces moved forward, the fighting in the Cornfield, West Woods, and at Sunken Road was almost finished.

Burnside's opening attack was supposed to be a coordinated three-prong assault. Three hundred soldiers from Connecticut were ordered to ford the creek several hundred feet south of the bridge. As this was taking this, the water was nearly chest-high. When Confederate snipers began firing at them, the Union troops withdrew and began searching for a better place to cross. Ordinarily, this would have been done by the fast-moving cavalry, but McClellan, fearing a massive Confederate counterattack, had ordered them to stay at headquarters. So Rodman's men had to stumble along the banks of the stream, hunting for a way across, all the time being shot at by enemy sharpshooters.

A second charge on the bridge was quickly assembled. This one consisted of three hundred soldiers from Maryland and New Hampshire led by Lieutenant Colonel Jacob Duryea. Duryea organized his men behind a small hill in a cornfield 250 yards south of the bridge. Their division surgeon, Dr. Theodore Dimon, located the Marylanders just as Duryea barked at his men to move forward in a line toward the road.

When they emerged from the protection of the hill, the Confederate sharpshooters across the creek went to work. At the same time, rebel artillery on high ground zeroed in on the line of blue. The withering combination of shot and shell shredded the line and men began falling left and right into the corn, the screams of the wounded drowned out by the rumbling boom of the cannons.

Those that survived soon reached the road and headed for the bridge. Duryea's men were now firing blindly into the trees across from them, though the dense leaf cover and clouds of bitter-smelling smoke made seeing the enemy nearly impossible. To find some protection for his men, Duryea led them off the road and immediately encountered a strongly constructed fence.

As Duryea and several men struggled to rip an opening through the fence, Dr. Dimon came up to them. Dimon saw Duryea look around. "The Regiment [was]

shrinking and elbowing out under the tremendous fire and just ready to break," Dimon recalled. Duryea screamed, "What the hell are you doing there? Straighten that line there! Forward!"

Duryea threw a section of fence aside and ran across a field of stubble and into a pasture that bordered the road, his men following closely on his heels. Several made it to the lower end of the bridge, but were stopped from crossing it by an eruption of artillery fire. The Confederates were ramming every available piece of metal into the barrels of their cannons, including a fifteen-inch-long piece of railroad track that just missed taking off the head of a New Hampshire soldier. Duryea's men then withdrew to the cover of a rocky knoll some one hundred yards from the road.

Another group of New Hampshire soldiers came through the cornfield and entered the road and were joined by several hundred Pennsylvania troops. The commander of the New Hampshire men, Colonel Edward Ferrero, decided that attacking the bridge amounted to suicide and wanted instead to ford the creek at a bend. He sent back for permission to cross the creek, but was denied it and told to lead his men toward the bridge. When he sent a second request, explaining that enemy fire was concentrated on the bridge, he was informed that the order to charge the bridge came directly from General Burnside.

Ferrero had his men form into an attack column and said, "It is General Burnside's special request that [we] take the bridge. Will you do it?"

But instead of a lusty cheer from his soldiers, there was silence. They had been watching a stream of wounded and mangled men being carried back to the field hospital, many of them missing hands or legs, and screaming

*Sergeant Thomas Jefferson Rushin and 180 other men from Georgia were about two hundred yards from the East Woods when a large force of Union soldiers came at them. Rushin was killed in the opening volley.*

*Burnside's Bridge is finally taken, while the fighting continues on the hills in the background.*

horribly. Then out of the silence came the lone voice of Corporal Lewis Patterson, "Will you give us our whiskey, Colonel, if we take it?" Several days before, Ferrero had cut off the Pennsylvanians' whiskey ration over some minor misconduct.

The frustrated colonel glared at his corporal and yelled, "Yes, by God! You shall have as much as you want, if you take the bridge. . . . If it is in the commissary or I have to send to New York to get it, and pay for it out of my own pocket; that is if I live to see you through it. Will you take it?" This time, his question received a bellowing "Yes" from his troops.

Instead of marching up the road, which would have made his men easy targets, Ferrero took them across the stubble field to behind the knoll. After taking a few minutes to regroup and form up into an attack column, they charged straight for the bridge, only to be met by a tremendous barrage of shot and shell.

As more and more men fell from the column, the officers realized they would never make it across the bridge in a single rush. They had the men take up defensive positions behind a small stone wall and picket fence running along the road nearby. Lieutenant George Washington Whitman remembered, "We were then ordered to halt and commence fireing, and the way we showered the lead across that creek was noboddys business."

The Confederate soldiers continued their deadly sniping, but they had been fighting for almost three hours by this time and ammunition was running low. In groups of twos and threes, men dropped from their tree perches and ran up the hill to locate spare cartridges. The moment the rebel firing slackened, Union troops were on their feet and rushing for the bridge.

Outnumbered and out of ammunition, Confederate officers called for a full retreat and soon all the defenders near the bridge were in flight. The New Hampshire and Pennsylvania troops poured across what would be renamed Burnside's Bridge and spread out through the thick woods beyond.

Some two miles south, the main Union force finally located a decent spot to cross the creek. Snavely's Ford was lightly defended and casualties were relatively few as a long line of blue coats waded across and began spreading out through the woods. Shortly after 1 p.m., the Union battle line stretched from Snavely's all the way up to the bridge.

The third phase of McClellan's plan was at last complete. General Burnside had his bridge, and a few days later, the Pennsylvanians received their well-deserved reward, a keg of good Irish whiskey.

*Twenty-one-year-old Union Lieutenant John Clark had been on sick leave for most of the summer and returned to duty just as McClellan set out for Maryland in September. Sometime during the afternoon Clark was shot and killed.*

*This panoramic sketch of the battlefield was
made from McClellan's headquarters.*

# ✦10✦
# Cemetery Hill

McClellan is our joy and pride,
Hurrah! boys, hurrah!
We'll stand by him, what e'er betide,
Hurrah! boys, hurrah!

He is the Gen'ral of our choice,
Oh, shout for him with ev'ry voice,
He will soon make our land rejoice,
Hurrah! boys, hurrah!
—"McClellan Is Our Man" by Charles Leighton, 1862

Once Union forces were across the creek, a curious lull settled over the entire battlefield. McClellan had wanted Burnside to press forward immediately and attempt to take Sharpsburg. Burnside was willing to do this, only he and all of his officers had forgotten a key item—ammunition. Apparently, no one had thought to bring the ammunition wagons up to speed distribution to the troops. The wagons had to now be ordered forward, causing serious delays.

Then Union General Samuel Sturgis decided his men across the creek were exhausted and couldn't press the fight any longer. No one—not Burnside or any other senior officer—thought to question this appraisal or even

to suggest that further delays would allow Lee to regroup and reposition troops. It would take more than two hours to bring up ammunition and replace Sturgis's troops.

Not that many of the soldiers minded. More than five hundred Union soldiers were killed taking the bridge, while 120 Confederate soldiers died defending it. "The sun seemed almost to go backwards," a Confederate from North Carolina wrote, "and it appeared as if night would never come." Alex Chisholm from Alabama remembered, "We were praying for night to come." Union soldier James Fowler kept hoping "that we might not be called upon again, and lo the luck of the 10th Maine was with us and we were undisturbed."

The fighting hadn't stopped completely. Occasional shots rang out as snipers spied the color of an enemy's uniform. Random shells were lobbed across the battle line. One shell exploded in the air above thirteen-year-old Charlie King from Pennsylvania, a flying piece of metal killing him instantly. Another landed in a street in Sharpsburg near a Confederate soldier and, as a soldier nearby reported, the force of the explosion made the man "turn over and over like a wagon wheel."

The lull in the fighting seemed to bother McClellan. He was convinced that Lee's counterattack was finally about to commence. But where on the field of battle would it happen? "All wore a serious air," Colonel Strother remembered as he observed the senior officers at headquarters. "From the signs of the day and the report of prisoners, it was evident the enemy was before us in full power, and the fact that he had risked a battle in his present position showed that he felt great confidence in his power."

Several Union officers suggested it would be a good time to charge the enemy's left flank, but all McClellan would order was that the lines be held. He had over 20,000 men in reserve, plus nearly 1,000 cavalry, but he wouldn't commit them to the fight, holding them out to deal with the imagined Confederate attack he was certain was about to be launched.

"Most of us think that this battle is only half fought and half won," twenty-five-year-old Lieutenant James Wilson told a reporter that day. "There is still time to finish it. But McClellan will do no more." A number of generals, including George Meade, Abner Doubleday, and Alpheus Williams, agreed that the fight should be renewed against the enemy's left flank, but they met stiff resistance from Little Mac and his staff.

After continued urging, McClellan went forward personally to check out the situation. McClellan located Bull Sumner and asked what the condition of his troops was. Sumner "expressed the most decided opinion against another attempt during that day." Sumner may have still been in shock over the beating his troops had taken in the West Woods, but McClellan, despite his doubts about Sumner's ability, never questioned his opinion. Instead, he abandoned completely the idea of attacking.

Lee, on the other hand, seemed remarkably calm when he surveyed the location of the enemy and his troops. While Union forces had crossed the Rohrbach Bridge, they hadn't pressed their advantage. And his troops to the north seemed to have fought the enemy to a standstill. He then decided on a bold plan to take the action to the enemy. He would send a force of 5,000 to circle around the enemy to the north and strike at them from the rear. When this happened, his soldiers in the West Woods would also attack, thus putting the Union troops in that section under fire from two directions.

To this point, Union General Ambrose Burnside had run what might at best be called a sloppy attack. Then at 3 p.m. General Burnside suddenly seemed to regain his focus on the fighting. That was when he ordered 8,000 additional men across the Rohrbach Bridge and Snavely's Ford with orders to drive the enemy back through the town of Sharpsburg.

The advancing line of blue snaked across open fields and pastures. The troops were clearly visible from the Pry house and Colonel Strother recalled the sight. "Burnside made his grand effort. His advancing rush was in full view and magnificently done."

Opposing this new Union challenge were just 2,800 Confederate troops, supported by twenty-eight pieces of artillery. The only advantage they had was the terrain. Rebel troops were on high ground positioned behind stone walls with a clear view of the advancing enemy across the plowed fields.

Troops from New York were in the lead, taking a road to the right of the bridge and easily routing the sparse rebel forces they encountered. The enemy fell back and back until it came to Cemetery Hill, where their artillery halted the Union charge. At this point the advantage of the high ground for the Confederates was felt. A rain of hot metal whirled into the stalled Union lines, shredding them. A sixteen-year-old new recruit in the lead group, Private William Brearley, wrote home to his father, "I have heard and seen pictures of battles—they would all be in line, all standing in a nice level field fighting, a number of ladies taking care of the wounded, &c &c. but it isent so."

The ground shook under Brearley's feet each time the artillery batteries fired. Shells arced screaming through the air to explode with thunderous claps. Bullets whirred overhead like angry hornets, clipping away cornstalks and tree branches. And men. The groans and screams of the wounded mixed uneasily with the *pop-pop-pop* of musketfire. "I had a bullet strike me on top of the head just as I was going to fire," Brearley recalled, "and a piece of Shell struck my foot—a ball hit my finger and another hit my thumb." The young soldier then ended his note dryly, "I concluded they ment [to shoot] me."

The Confederate artillery on Cemetery Hill came in for heavy fire from the long-range Union Parrott guns some two miles away. One rebel gun took a direct hit that splintered its barrel and killed all the men there. A second was disabled when its carriage was hit. As ammunition ran out, one by one the guns were hauled away

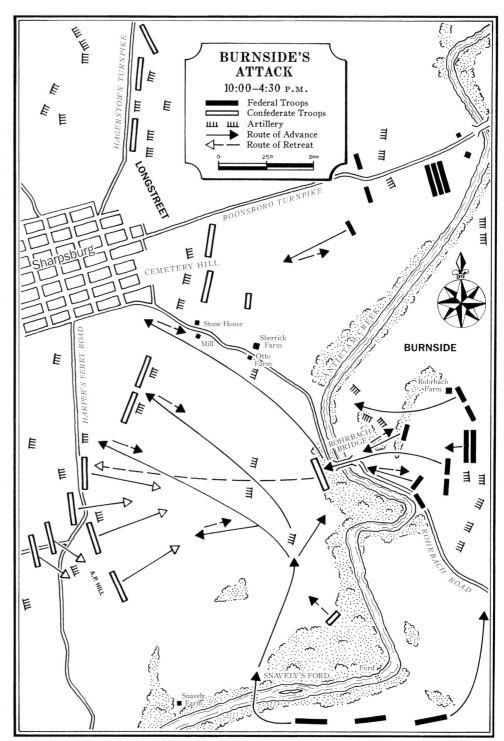

**BURNSIDE'S ATTACK**

10:00–4:30 P.M.

Federal Troops
Confederate Troops
Artillery
Route of Advance
Route of Retreat

0        250        500

*Soldiers from New York (in the foreground) are beginning to drive the Confederate soldiers back into the town of Sharpsburg.*

by hand, hitched to waiting horses and hastily driven through town so they wouldn't fall into enemy hands.

Desperate hand-to-hand bayonet fighting dislodged the Confederates holding a mill and stone house near Cemetery Hill, while Union cannons blasted away at an apple orchard, until the soldiers there had to withdraw. For a time, Confederate artillery in the cemetery slowed the Union troops down, forcing them to sprint short distances, find cover, and wait for the next opportunity to advance.

The soldiers from New York were less than a half mile from the roaring guns on Cemetery Hill when the order to charge was given. Private David Thompson leaped to his feet and began running forward, his heart beating so fast that his vision blurred and "the whole landscape for an instant turned slightly red."

A man just in front of Thompson suddenly threw up his hands and called out that he'd been hit. To Thompson's right, a shell exploded, killing eight of his comrades instantly. Solid shot from the cannons bounded along the fields, tearing up chunks of earth and severing the arms and legs of those in the way. Nearly one-quarter of all the New York troops—240 men—were killed or injured in the opening few moments of the charge.

The men halted briefly in a shallow depression beyond the road and organized themselves to renew the charge. "Bully, Ninth! Bully, Ninth," shouted their colonel, Edgar Kimball, "I'm proud of you! Every one of you!"

Heavy fire ate away at the wood fence near their position, then a mighty explosion ripped a wide gap in it. Colonel Kimball was on his feet again, yelling, "Get up the Ninth!"

No one responded and Lieutenant Matthew Graham thought the colonel had become unhinged. They wouldn't last but a few seconds if they charged straight at the rebel battery. But Kimball was dead serious. "Get up the Ninth!" he roared again. This time they responded, running through the section of ripped-up fence, screaming and cursing as they sprinted up toward the battery of deadly cannon.

A rebel gunner looked down the slope and saw the swarm of Union soldiers coming toward him as thick "as Pharaoh's locusts." As the Union troops drew nearer to the Confederate lines, the long-range cannon of both sides ceased firing, fearing they would hit their own troops. In the sudden silence, the sound of shouted commands and the encouraging calls of soldiers was what carried through the air as seven hundred New Yorkers closed in on some six hundred Confederate soldiers from Virginia, Georgia, and South Carolina.

Private Alexander Hunter of Virginia waited with a feeling of doom for the enemy to appear above a rise of land. "Our brigade was a mere outline of its former strength, not a sixth remaining. Our regiment, the Seventeenth, that once carried into battle eight hundred muskets, now stood on the crest, ready to die in a forlorn hope, with but forty-six muskets. . . ."

On came the wave of blue on the double-quick. "The first thing we saw appear," Hunter would remember, "was the gilt eagle that surmounted the pole, then the top of the flag, next the flutter of the stars and stripes itself, slowly mounting, up it rose, then their hats came in sight, still rising the faces emerged, next a range of curious eyes appeared, then such a hurrah as only the Yankee troops could give, broke the stillness, and they surged against us." Scarcely one hundred feet separated the two groups when each side unleashed a deadly fire.

The fighting became a frantic exercise of firing, reloading, and firing again. Some took careful aim, while many simply fired in a panic, their shots flying wide of the target. The seconds it took to load must have felt like a lifetime to the soldiers on both sides.

The Confederate troops stood up to the Union troops for as long as possible, but eventually the enemy's superior numbers took a toll and a general retreat was called. John Dooley of Virginia left the cemetery and scampered toward the rear, though he was acutely aware that he might be seen as a coward. "I was afraid of being struck in the *back*," he would write, "and I frequently turned half around in running, so as to avoid if possible so disgraceful a wound."

Confederate troops, horse-drawn artillery, and ambulances were soon streaming through the narrow streets of Sharpsburg in complete disarray. One woman recalled seeing an ambulance fly past her, a trail of blood dripping out the floorboards and someone inside wailing in pain, "O Lord! O Lord! O Lord!"

*Confederate Lieutenant John Dooley was so worried about receiving a "coward's wound" in the back that he ran backward while retreating.*

McClellan and his staff watched all of this from headquarters with a growing sense that complete victory was within their grasp. A message came from General Burnside requesting that McClellan release the reserve troops he'd promised to support Burnside's advance. Military logic suggested this was a sensible course of action: the enemy was wavering and retreating and the best way to speed the rout along was with overwhelming force. Besides, McClellan had promised Burnside that he would support his attack when the time came. McClellan was about to give the command to send in the reserves when Fitz John Porter reminded him that Lee might counterattack at any moment. The order was never given.

Meanwhile, General Lee joined his staff officers in trying to halt the chaotic retreat, but had little luck. Soon Union artillery commenced firing into the town, striking the Lutheran church on Main Street several times. The church had been turned into a temporary hospital, and surgeon J. R. Boulware angrily recalled dust and debris flying about him. "I never was so tired of shelling in my life before," he noted. "I *hate cannons*."

The Confederate lines on the right were collapsing. Once Union forces had secured this section, they could wheel around and drive the depleted Southern troops in the north from their positions. The force Lee had sent to circle around Union forces there had been halted in thick woods far to the north and were out of the fight for the rest of the day.

Lee rode to his headquarters to observe the deteriorating situation off to his right. Another hour of fighting and his men there would break completely and his campaign would be shattered. That was when he noticed soldiers to the south and asked a young officer with a telescope what troops they were. "They are flying the Virginia and Confederate flag," the officer replied.

Lee nodded his head and said simply, "That is A. P. Hill from Harper's Ferry."

General Ambrose Powell Hill was a man with a fiery personality that seemed to match his tangled hair and red beard. Hill had driven his 3,200 troops at a frantic pace, at times using the flat of his sword to keep men moving, and managed to cover the seventeen miles from Harper's Ferry in less than eight hours. When he arrived, he did not even halt his men to organize them for the fight as most generals would have done. Sensing the desperate position the Army of Northern Virginia was in, Hill rushed artillery and soldiers into battle as they came on the scene.

The result of Burnside's delayed attack and McClellan's refusal to send in the promised reserves was that A. P. Hill appeared at just the right time and in just the right place. Hill's cannons opened on the advancing Yankee lines, followed by a massed charge of screaming Confederate soldiers.

"Things began to look rather squally," Union Lieutenant George Washington Whitman would remember. "Our Regt fired every round of ammunition we had, and took from all the dead and wounded on the field and then we lay down as we would not leave the field untill we were ordered."

But the momentum had shifted, and the Union troops now found themselves outgunned and outmaneuvered. They held their positions for as long as possible, then began pulling back slowly. A regimental historian recalled that "even the chaplain snatches the rifle and cartridge-box of a dead man, and fights for life."

At 4:30, McClellan sent Burnside a desperate message. "Tell General Burnside this is the battle of the war. He must hold his ground till dark at any cost. . . . Tell him if he cannot hold his ground, then the bridge, to the last man!—always the bridge! If the bridge is lost, all is lost!"

The fight was gone from McClellan, if indeed he ever had it in him. He was willing to settle for what amounted to a tactical draw, having gained a little bit of ground but not driving the enemy from its strong defensive positions. As the sun began to set and the light dimmed, the sounds of fighting faded. "Gradually the thunder dies," wrote Charles Coffin of the *Boston Journal*. "The flashes are fewer. The musketry ceases and silence comes on, broken only by an occasional volley, and single shots, like the last drops of a shower."

*Confederate General A. P. Hill got his men and artillery onto the Antietam battlefield in time to halt the Union charge.*

The Battle of Antietam had come to a sputtering end, and now it was time for another sort of brigade to go into action. When the smoke cleared and shooting finally stopped, the stretcher-bearers and burial crews emerged to begin their grim work.

⊷•◦•⬥•◦•⊶

CEMETERY HILL 71

# ★ 11 ★
# The Smell of Death

The foul-beaked vultures, sated, flap their wings
O'er crowded corpses, that but yesterday
Bore hearts of brother, beating high with love
And common hopes and pride, all blasted now—
—"A Prayer for Peace" by Severn Teackle Wallis,
written sometime during the war

No sooner had the fighting stopped than stretcher-bearers, medical orderlies, and soldiers began searching the torn-up fields and tangled woods for dead and wounded comrades. A Confederate officer thought that "half of Lee's army was hunting the other half."

All of this took place behind each army's battle lines, where there was less chance of being shot by a nervous foe. This left thousands of wounded trapped between the opposing lines in a dangerous no man's land. "This was a miserable night for me," a member of a Union artillery battery remembered. "Groans and cries for water could be heard the whole night. We could not help them."

Captain William G. LaDuc of Massachusetts was shocked to literally stumble upon his close friend, Captain Oliver Wendell Holmes Jr., whom he thought had been killed. Holmes could barely talk because of the gaping wound he'd suffered to his neck, but he was alive. No surgeons were available, so LaDuc cleaned and bandaged the wound himself. "The Captain squirmed a little under my surgery," LaDuc recalled, "and said I'm glad LaDuc it aint a case for amputation for I have duced little confidence in your surgery." After patching up his friend as best as he could, LaDuc got Holmes to the closest hospital, then he telegraphed a terse message to his friend's father, the famous author Dr. Oliver Wendell Holmes Sr., which said, "Capt. Holmes shot wounded through the neck thought not mortal."

Churches, barns, and sheds were turned into field hospitals, and surgeons began the nightmarish task of treating ghastly injuries. A Southern newspaperman, Peter Alexander, glanced into one of these places and was nearly sick with what he encountered. "There is a smell of death in the air," he recalled, "and the surgeons are literally covered from head to foot with the blood of

*Citizen Volunteers Assisting the wounded on the field of Battle* ........ *A G R Waud*

Civilians helping to remove wounded soldiers from the battlefield. On the left,
surgeons have just removed a portion of a soldier's right leg.

the sufferers." Pits were dug nearby where amputated hands, feet, and limbs were dumped and hastily buried.

Thirty-six hours after being shot, Mary Galloway was found by friendly troops and brought to the nearest hospital, where she had to wait another twenty-four hours before a doctor came to check her wounds. The bullet that had pierced her neck had traveled downward and across her body, lodging in the right side of her back. Without any sort of painkiller, the doctor used a long metal clamp to dig out the bullet. Galloway later recovered and was able to locate her boyfriend in a hospital in Frederick.

Eventually, fifty-seven makeshift hospitals would be set up in Sharpsburg and surrounding villages, each packed with the wounded. One local woman remembered that injured soldiers "filled every building and overflowed into the country round, into farm-houses, barns, corn-cribs, cabins—wherever four walls and a roof were found. Those able to travel were sent to Winchester and other towns back from the river, but their departure seemed to make no appreciable difference."

It would take weeks before a proper count of the casualties could be made. The numbers only confirmed the horror that the men in battle had witnessed. McClellan's Army of the Potomac suffered 2,108 killed, 9,540 wounded, and 753 missing (most of whom were presumed to be dead) for a total of 12,401 men. Lee's casualties were estimated at 1,546 killed, 7,752 wounded, and 1,018 missing, which came to 10,316 men. The total for both sides—22,717 casualties—meant that the twelve hours of battle at Antietam would be the bloodiest single day of fighting in American history.

That night, Lee called a meeting of his senior officers. Nearly one-third of his men were injured or dead.

He had no prospects of receiving fresh recruits, either. Yet his only orders were to rearrange some of the artillery, round up stragglers, and issue hot rations to troops in the forward line. He and his battered army of 30,000 were going to stay and fight on September 18.

McClellan, on the other hand, was apprehensive. He still believed he was outnumbered by Lee's army, still worried that a massive counterattack could cut his army in half and doom the Union. In fact, he had a vastly larger force than Lee. McClellan had nearly 30,000 troops on the field, with 26,300 in reserve nearby, while another 13,000 were expected to arrive in a matter of hours. Still, he could not bring himself to commit to a decisive battle that might have ended the war. "A careful and anxious survey of the condition of my command," he would later explain, "and my knowledge of the enemy's forces and position, failed to impress me with any reasonable certainty of success if I renewed the attack without re-enforcing columns."

The eighteenth of September dawned, but McClellan did not initiate a fight. As the day wore on, soldiers on both sides called truces so they could retrieve the wounded stranded between the battle lines. Burial details continued their work as well. Colonel Strother rode to the East Woods to check on his men there. "In the midst of all this carrion, our troops sat cooking, eating, jabbering, and smoking; sleeping among the corpses so that but for the color of the skin it was difficult to distinguish the living from the dead."

As the sun went down, Lee sent a message to Confederate president Jefferson Davis: "Though still too weak to assume the offensive, we awaited without apprehension the renewal of the attack. The day passed without any demonstration on the part of the enemy." Later that

*Barns, houses, huts, corn cribs, and chicken coops were all used as temporary hospitals. While the wounded look on, surgeons operate on one of their injured comrades.*

night, Lee reconsidered his decision to linger near the Union army and the order was given to withdraw from Sharpsburg.

Lee had no intention of calling off his campaign, however, and even drew up a new plan to recross the Potomac at Williamsport and invade Maryland again. But he soon discovered an obstacle more formidable than the Union army. His men were worn out and demoralized. As Brigadier General Dorsey Pender told his wife, "Some of the Army have a fight nearly every day, and the more we fight, the less we like it." Hundreds of men simply left their comrades and headed for home. On September 25, a reluctant General Lee had to inform Davis that his campaign was officially over: "I would not hesitate to [initiate an attack] even with our diminished numbers, did the army exhibit its former temper and condition; but, as far as I am able to judge, the hazard would be great and a reverse disastrous. I am, therefore, led to pause."

McClellan was more than happy to see the Confederate army withdraw. For him, this amounted to proof that he'd accomplished a complete and unquestionable victory. He may have hesitated on the field of battle, but he did not hesitate to proclaim victory and take his bows. In a message to Ellen, he crowed, "I feel some little pride in having, with a beaten and demoralized army, defeated Lee so utterly and saved the North so completely. . . . I have the satisfaction of knowing that God has, in his mercy, a second time made me the instrument for saving the nation."

He then sent a message to General Halleck. "Our victory was complete. The enemy is driven back into Virginia. Maryland and Pennsylvania are now safe."

History and many of his own troops didn't agree with his appraisal. A captain from Maine wrote in disgust, "We should have followed them up the next day," while a Connecticut officer could "imagine no earthly reason why we did not go at them . . . with a vengeance." Colonel Thomas Welsh found himself "thoroughly disgusted with the management of this army. . . . The whole Rebel Army could have been captured or destroyed easily before it could have crossed the Potomac—but indeed it seems to me that McClellan let them escape purposely."

The frustration in Washington was, if anything, even greater. Four days before, Lincoln had expressly told McClellan to "destroy the rebel army, if possible." And according to all the reports he was receiving in Washington, it had been within McClellan's grasp—and yet it hadn't happened. "Nothing from the army," said the Secretary of the Navy, Gideon Wells, "except that, instead of following up the victory, attacking and capturing the Rebels, they . . . are rapidly escaping across the river. . . . Oh dear."

Both Abraham Lincoln and Henry Halleck urged McClellan to pursue Lee, but to no avail. His army was tired, McClellan would explain, and needed to rest. Ammunition and shoes were in short supply. Horses and wagons were urgently needed. When two weeks of McClellan's foot-dragging and excuses became too much for Lincoln to bear, he went to the battlefield to talk to his general in person.

McClellan knew precisely why Lincoln had come to see him. "I incline to think," he told Ellen, "that the real purpose of his visit is to push me into a premature advance into Virginia."

Lincoln did urge him to advance and even suggested, according to his friend, Judge David Davis, that "he [McClellan] wd be a ruined man if he did not move

forward, move rapidly & effectively." But when Lincoln returned to Washington four days later, he was still frustrated. "I went up to the field to try to get him to move & came back thinking he would move at once. But when I got home he began to argue why he ought not to move."

On October 6, Halleck sent McClellan an urgent dispatch stating that the president ordered him to "cross the Potomac and give battle to the enemy. . . . Your army must move now, while the roads are good."

McClellan responded that Lee's army was "undoubtedly greatly superior" in numbers to his, and that unless he received reinforcements, "I may have too much on my hands in the next battle."

A week later, Lincoln wrote to McClellan himself. "You remember my speaking to you of what I called your over-cautiousness? Are you not over-cautious when you assume that you can not do what the enemy is constantly doing? Should you not claim to be at least his equal in prowess, and act upon the claim?"

*The Army of North Virginia makes its escape.*

McClellan still would not engage the enemy. He allowed his army to sit and idle away its time even as Confederate General Jeb Stuart took 1,800 cavalrymen and rode completely around McClellan's army to gather up 1,200 horses and other badly needed supplies. He would not move even when Lincoln prodded him again and again. "I would press closely to [Lee]," Lincoln advised him, "fight him if a favorable opportunity should present, and, at least, try to beat him to Richmond. . . . I say 'try'; if we never try, we shall never succeed." And when McClellan responded that his cavalry horses were fatigued, Lincoln snapped back, "Will you pardon me for asking what the horses of your army have done since the battle of Antietam that fatigues anything?"

In fact, McClellan's stalling had become a personal statement to show Lincoln and his cabinet exactly who was in charge of the army. Once he wrote to Ellen to denounce Lincoln, Halleck, and others for pushing and insulting him since they were "men whom I know to be greatly my inferior socially, intellectually & morally!" Then, making a reference to Lincoln, he concluded, "There never was a truer epithet applied to a certain individual than that of the 'Gorilla.'"

On October 26, nearly six weeks after the Battle of Antietam, McClellan finally got his army up and marching again. Moving very slowly, the Army of the Potomac—now with almost 100,000 soldiers—took eight days to cross the Potomac and advance twenty miles into Virginia. But it was already too late to destroy Lee's Army of Northern Virginia. Left alone in the Shenandoah Valley, Lee's army had rested and regained its fighting spirit. Stragglers were rounded up and brought back into camp. Volunteers began arriving from Richmond and other points south. By October 10,

the number of healthy men Lee had in camp had increased to over 64,000—double the number he had when he left Sharpsburg.

In early November, Lee sent a portion of his troops to get between Richmond and McClellan's army. Once again, the Army of the Potomac halted and did nothing. For Lincoln, this was "the last grain of sand which broke the camel's back." He sent a message to General Halleck: "By direction of the President, it is ordered that Major General McClellan be relieved from the command of the Army of the Potomac; and that Major General Burnside take the command of that Army."

Little Mac would never in his lifetime admit to any errors of judgment, either during the Battle of Antietam or afterward. "Of course I was much surprised," he confided to Ellen after receiving word that he had been replaced, "but as I read the order in the presence of Gen. Buckingham I am sure that not the slightest expression was visible on my face, which he watched closely. They shall not have that triumph. They have made a great mistake. Alas for my poor country!" He then concluded, "Our consolation must be that we have tried to do what was right; if we have failed it was not our fault."

While the drama between Abraham Lincoln and George McClellan was playing out, the reality of the September battle along Antietam Creek was beginning to sink in. Samuel Fiske, a clergyman attached to a Connecticut brigade, wrote a letter that appeared in the *Springfield Republican*. "The excitement of battle comes in the day of it, but the horrors of it two or three days after." He then described the hundreds of bodies strewn about the fields, blackened and bloated. "Think now of the horrors of such a scene as lies all around us. . . . There are hundreds of [dead] horses, too, all mangled

*President Lincoln meets with McClellan after the Battle of Antietam. A frustrated Lincoln would urge his commander to rally his troops and strike at Lee's retreating army, but to no avail.*

553.      The "Sunken Road" at Antietam.
[FOR DESCRIPTION OF THIS VIEW SEE THE OTHER SIDE OF THIS CARD.]

*Piles of dead Confederate soldiers in the Sunken Road.*

and putrifying, scattered everywhere! Then there are the broken gun-carriages, the wagons, and thousands of muskets, and all sorts of equipments, and clothing all torn and bloody, and cartridges and cannon-shot, and pieces of shell, the trees torn with shot and scarred with bullets, the farm-houses and barns knocked to pieces and burned down, the crops trampled and wasted, the whole country forlorn and desolate."

No sooner had the Confederate forces withdrawn than two men appeared in the northern section of the battlefield. They were Alexander Gardner and his assistant, James F. Gibson, photographers for Mathew Brady's Photographic Company. Slowly, methodically, they set up their large camera and took photographs of the carnage they discovered. It was the first time in American history that a battlefield was photographed before the dead had been buried.

In the days that followed, the work of burying the dead and caring for the wounded went on. With the Confederate army gone, Union troops were able to organize large burial details to clear the farms of bodies. One man described how his group advanced across the fields as if in line of battle, collecting bodies and dragging them to the designated burial site. "When the Pit is dug deep enough the Bodies are placed crosswise and as many as fourty seven in one Grave. After the Union men were all gathered up and buried then we commenced gathering up the Rebs. . . . We seen among the rebels Boys of Sixteen & Fifteen and old Grey headed men."

While a mass grave was the usual fate for Confederate soldiers, at least one was accorded special treatment. While dragging bodies to a pit, Private Mark Nickerson was startled to discover a woman among the Confederate dead. "The news soon spread among the soldiers," he recalled, "and many of them went and gazed upon the upturned face, tears glistening in many eyes. . . . She was wrapped in a soldier's blanket and buried by herself and a head board made from a cracker box was set up at her grave marked 'unknown Woman CSA.'"

Scores of friends and relatives began arriving at the battlefield to look for missing relatives. Dr. Oliver Wendell Holmes arrived in Frederick late on September 19 and immediately set out for Sharpsburg in search of his wounded son. He was appalled by what he saw from the road. "There was something repulsive about the trodden and stained relics of the stale battlefield," he would write. "It was like the table of some hideous orgy left uncleared, and one turned away disgusted from its broken fragments. . . ."

Because no one had recorded where individual soldiers were being cared for, Dr. Holmes had to go from hospital to hospital, stopping at every bed to see if it held his son. "Many times . . . I started as some faint resemblance—the shade of a young man's hair, the

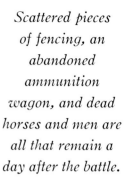

*Scattered pieces of fencing, an abandoned ammunition wagon, and dead horses and men are all that remain a day after the battle.*

outline of his half-turned face—recalled the presence I was in search of." Finally, he traced his son to Hagerstown and was lucky enough to arrive minutes before a train loaded with wounded soldiers was about to leave. "In the first car, on the fourth seat to the right, I saw my Captain. . . ."

Dr. Holmes was one of the lucky ones. Too often, however, these searches had sad endings. A friend of a family whose son had been wounded in the Cornfield wrote to inform them that he had died six days later. He knew that the tragic news would upset the family terribly, and in plain language he tried to reassure them

that their boy's burial had been as decent and as loving as possible: "I bought a rough coffin (the best I could get) and washed his face and combed his hair and covered him round with a large clean sheet. And they dug a deep grave on a little knoll on the bank of the Antietam Creek, and I buried him there. I marked the place . . . by a board neatly made at his head with his initials."

In October, Matthew Brady held an exhibit in his New York City studio of the photographs Gardner and Gibson had made of the battlefield. Entitled "The Dead of Antietam," the exhibit attracted thousands of people who had never heard the roar of cannons or seen the clash

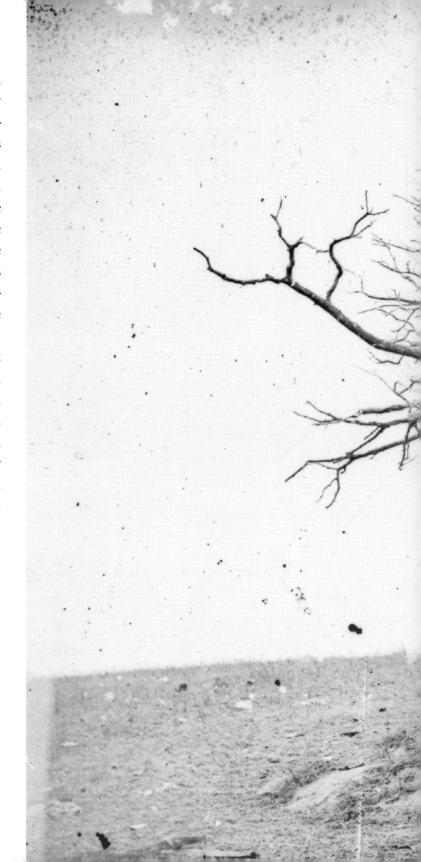

*A lone grave at the base of a tree.*

of two great armies. The effect on viewers was stunning, as a reporter for the *New York Times* noted. "Mr. Brady has done something to bring home to us the terrible reality and earnestness of war. If he has not brought bodies and laid them in our door-yards and along the streets, he has done something very like it." If he had a criticism of the photographs, it was this: "There is one side of the picture that . . . has escaped photographic skill. It is the background of the widows and orphans. . . . Homes have been made desolate, and the light of life in thousands of hearts has been quenched forever. All of this desolation imagination must paint—broken hearts cannot be photographed."

The thunder of battle had given way to the quiet of a vast, rolling graveyard. The men buried there had fought for their countries and their way of life, and paid the ultimate price for their strong and earnest beliefs. Now it was time for the living to mourn those who would never again come home and for the poets to recall their memory. One of the most famous poems to be published after the war was Francis Miles Finch's "The Blue and the Gray."

By the flow of the inland river,
    Whence the fleets of iron have fled,
Where the blades of the grave-grass quiver,
    Asleep are the ranks of the dead:
Under the sod and the dew,
    Waiting the Judgment Day:
Under the one, the Blue,
    Under the other, the Gray.

# ⋆12⋆
# Emancipation

I break your bonds and masterships,
And I unchain the slave;
Free be his heart and hand henceforth
As wind and wandering wave.
—"Boston Hymn" by Ralph Waldo Emerson, 1863

Almost as soon as the shooting stopped in Sharpsburg another battle began—a battle of words. On September 21, the *New York Sunday Mercury* exclaimed, "When we recollect what a transition has taken place, from the depth of despondency to the height of exultation, from defeat to glorious victory, we ought to rejoice over what has been done. . . ." The *New York Times* ran a giant headline that proclaimed GREAT VICTORY, saying the Battle of Antietam "must take its place among the grand decisive conflicts of history."

Because Lee did not have a telegraph link to the south, people there first learned the details of the battle from Northern newspapers. Naturally, the Southern press strongly disagreed with their Northern rivals' opinions of the battle. The *Richmond Enquirer* dismissed the claims of a Union victory as "sheer and shameless fabrication . . . monstrous fables . . . nauseating absurdities." The *Richmond Dispatch* was indignant that "our

community should have been so excited by the lying reports of the Yankee papers." It pointed out that 13,000 Federal soldiers had been captured at Harper's Ferry and that Lee had fought a numerically superior Union army to a standstill and then withdrawn from Maryland in a calm and unhurried fashion. It then logically concluded, "If we have been thus badly beaten, why is no use made of the victory? Why has McClellan not crossed the river and destroyed the army of Gen. Lee? Why has the latter been allowed to refresh and recruit at his leisure? The truth is this: The victory, though not so decisive as that of Manassas, was certainly a Confederate victory."

The squabbling over bragging rights to a "victory" would continue for many years. Even today, historians debate the way Lee and McClellan managed their troops on September 17, picking apart each decision and rating their every move, big and little. What is clear is that the Battle of Antietam was a turning point in the war

*President Lincoln reading the Emancipation Proclamation to his cabinet.*

that not only helped determine the eventual outcome of the fighting but forever changed the lives of millions of people.

On September 22, Abraham Lincoln called his cabinet together for a special meeting. After discussing a book by Artemus Ward and reading a chapter from it, the president took on "a graver tone," as Secretary of the Treasury Salmon Chase recalled.

Lincoln reminded them that back in July he had agreed to postpone issuing the Emancipation Proclamation until the Union achieved a military victory in the field. "I wish it was a better time. . . . The action of the army against the rebels has not been quite what I should have best liked. But they have been driven out of Maryland." He went on to tell them that when Lee was in Frederick, he had decided, "that if God gave us the victory in the approaching battle, [I] would consider it an indication of Divine Will" to issue the Proclamation. Lincoln paused a moment, then said quietly, "God [has] decided this question in favor of the slaves."

The Emancipation Proclamation is a legal document and as such is not as eloquent as many of Lincoln's speeches. In formal, legal language it states where authority to confiscate enemy property came from and then issues a warning: If the rebelling states did not return to the Union within one hundred days, on January 1, 1863, all individuals held as slaves in those states "shall be then, thenceforward, and forever free. . . ."

The next day, the Proclamation was released to the newspapers, while 15,000 copies were printed for distribution to Union troops. In Southern areas under Union control, many officers took their copy of the Proclamation and read it to assembled African Americans.

Reaction to the Proclamation was swift. Political opponents denounced President Lincoln as being "adrift on the current of radical fanaticism." The *New York Journal of Commerce* warned Lincoln not to expect "his new policy to be supported by the conservative men of the country, who believe it to be unconstitutional and wrong."

Others, however, supported the move wholeheartedly. The publisher of the *New York Tribune*, Horace Greeley, was ecstatic when he wrote the headline GOD BLESS ABRAHAM LINCOLN! predicting that freeing the slaves would be "the beginning of the end of the rebellion; the beginning of a new life of the nation." Senator Charles Sumner echoed this sentiment when he said "the skies are brighter and the air is purer, now that slavery has been handed over to judgment." Frederick Douglass probably voiced the emotions of many African Americans when he said, "We shout for joy that we live to record this righteous decree."

The reaction in the Union army was just as strong. Many soldiers who had enlisted to preserve the Union were not happy to be fighting to free the slaves. One soldier griped that "the men are all exasperated against the Tribune and would hang Greeley if they had their way," adding that "They do not wish to think that they are fighting for Negroes. . . ."

Several senior officers expressed their anger as well. General Fitz John Porter wrote to the editor of the anti-Lincoln *New York World* that the Emancipation Proclamation "was resented in the army—caused disgust, discontent, and expressions of disloyalty. . . ." He then claimed that the hard work of the military was being undermined "by the absurd proclamation of a political coward who . . . holds in his hands the lives of thousands and trifles with them."

THE EFFECTS OF THE PROCLAMATION—FREED NEGROES COMING INTO OUR LINES AT NEWBERN, NORTH CAROLINA.—[See Page 119.]

*Following the issuance of the Emancipation Proclamation in January 1863, former slaves make their way to the Union lines— and freedom.*

For several days, there was real fear that massive numbers of officers and soldiers might walk away from the fight, or worse, stage a rebellion that would result in a military dictator. One young officer, Lieutenant Edgar Newcomb, was quick to offer a candidate: "If McClellan wished to establish himself Supreme Dictator to-day, the army in the heat of their resentment of this wrong would be with him."

In the end, what anger there was subsided, and the army went back to the business at hand. As Colonel Charles Wainwright suggested, "Doubtless [rebellion] would have been the way were we French or German, but our people are naturally too law abiding." Even McClellan, who considered the Proclamation "infamous" and called Lincoln's administration a "despotism," never denounced it publicly. And there were soldiers who welcomed the Proclamation. One New England soldier wrote home proudly, "I do not intend to shirk now there is really something to fight for. I mean *Freedom*. . . ."

In England, news of the Emancipation Proclamation

brought a chorus of shouts from the press there. The *Glasgow Herald* felt it was "the last resort of a bewildered statesman," while the *London Standard* called it "the wretched makeshift of a pettifogging lawyer." But such criticisms were not held by the majority of Europeans. The *London Morning Star* may have been speaking for them when it declared the Proclamation "a gigantic stride in the paths of Christian and civilized progress—the turning point in the history of the American commonwealth—an act only second in courage and probable results to the Declaration of Independence."

While debate about the Proclamation went on in the press, another important matter was finally resolved. Two days before news about Antietam made it to London, the son-in-law of England's prime minister confided to Confederate envoys that "the event you so strongly desire, is very close at hand." The British and French governments were about to diplomatically recognize the Confederacy and offer to mediate an honorable end to the conflict. Then word of the fighting at Antietam arrived.

The prime minister read the dispatches and realized that the South had been dealt a severe blow. When, several days later, he learned about the Emancipation Proclamation, the fate of British–French intervention was sealed. "I am therefore inclined to change the opinion I wrote you when the Confederates seemed to be carrying all before them," he wrote the foreign secretary, Lord John Russell, "I am [convinced] . . . that we must continue to be lookers-on till the war shall have taken a more decided turn."

The situation would never change enough in the South's favor to prompt foreign intervention. Meanwhile, the Union blockade would grow ever more efficient, choking off Confederate revenue—and its ability to pay for food and supplies—for the rest of the war.

The Proclamation also changed the nature of the war. Before it was issued, the Union's objective had been to persuade the Confederate States that they could not win and should therefore negotiate for peace. Such a negotiation would have probably allowed them to keep the institution of slavery for a limited amount of time.

No one seriously believed that the Confederacy would willingly return to the Union in the time allotted in the Proclamation. For one thing, Lee had not been whipped thoroughly enough to persuade the South that they couldn't eventually defeat the North. And once the Proclamation became law, the South would have to fight to win or risk losing its slaves. "There is no possible hope of reconciliation," Commander-in-Chief Halleck told General Ulysses S. Grant. "We must conquer the rebels or be conquered by them. . . ."

There would be other "Antietams" during the two and a half years that remained of the Civil War. More than anyone involved could imagine. Tens of thousands of Union and Confederate soldiers would fall as casualties at Gettysburg, the Wilderness, Spotsylvania Court House, Cold Harbor, Cedar Creek, Petersburg, and Sailor's Creek, to name just a few. Before the war came to a bloody end with the Union victory at Appomattox Court House in April 1865, more than 475,000 Federal and Confederate soldiers would be wounded, while a staggering 625,000 men from both sides would die. How many fewer would have died or suffered hideous lifelong wounds if only McClellan had been less tentative will never be known.

What had begun as a war to maintain the United States had turned into a war to free the country's most helpless individuals, the nearly four and a half million men, women, and children being held as slaves. In the weeks and months following the issuance of the Emancipation Proclamation, tens of thousands of African Americans fled to the safety of the Union army. Many would offer their services to the officers and soldiers; they cooked meals, cleaned clothes, or did other manual chores. Some were paid for their work, while most received only their meals and a bed. What was important to them was that they did this work as free men and women and not as forced labor.

And when the Union army finally allowed African Americans to serve in the military in combat units, more than 186,000 freed slaves would enlist and fight to preserve the Union and destroy the chains of slavery. Sixty-eight thousand would add their names to the endless lists of those who died fighting to preserve their country and a Constitution that promised that "All men are created equal."

While the Emancipation Proclamation would have limited immediate impact, it may have done something even more important. It offered the millions of people still held in bondage something they had never had before—the hope that their futures would be blessed with freedom.

━●◆●◆●━

*Like most other soldiers, one of the first things that Sergeant J. L. Baldwin did after enlisting was to have his picture taken for loved ones back home.*

# NOTES AND SOURCES

## Preface

Lee's note to Jefferson Davis and Halleck's order to McClellan were found in James V. Murfin, *The Gleam of Bayonets: The Battle of Antietam and the Maryland Campaign of 1862* (Modern Library Editions Publishing Company, NY, 1965), pp. 61 and 76.

While I frequently use the word "men" when referring to soldiers, it's important to remember that between 200 and 400 women bore arms and served with bravery and honor during the Civil War. To date, eight women are known to have been combatants in the Battle of Antietam, including Sarah Edmonds, Catherine Davidson, Ida Remington, and Mary Galloway (who was only sixteen) for the Union. One woman is known to have fought for the Confederate side, but was never identified. Two books offer a detailed discussion of women combatants: DeAnne Blanton and Lauren M. Cook, *They Fought Like Demons: Women Soldiers in the Civil War* (Vintage Books, NY, 2003); and Mary Elizabeth Massey, *Women in the Civil War* (University of Nebraska Press, Lincoln, NE, 1966).

Frederick Douglass's quote appeared in *Douglass' Monthly* 4 (July 1861), p. 486.

## 1. Invasion

Singer-songwriter Henry Russell's 1861 song "The Southern Boys" (also known as "Cheer, Boys, Cheer") used youthful bravado, the defense of family and home, and a commitment to duty to help recruit soldiers for the Confederate cause. From E. Lawrence Abel, *Singing the New Nation: How Music Shaped the Confederacy, 1861–1865* (Stackpole Books, Mechanicsburg, PA, 2000), p. 17.

Detailed discussions of the actual invasion can be found in Joseph L. Harsh, *Taken at the Flood: Robert E. Lee & Confederate Strategy in the Maryland Campaign of 1861* (The Kent State University Press, Kent, OH, 1999), pp. 66–99; Stephen W. Sears, *Landscape Turned Red: The Battle of Antietam* (Ticknor & Fields, New Haven, CT, 1983), pp. 69–73 and 77–84; and Murfin, *The Gleam of Bayonets*, pp. 89–101.

The use of slaves as a military workforce and as an issue in domestic politics and foreign relations is nicely covered in James M. McPherson, *Antietam: The Battle That Changed the Course of the Civil War* (Oxford University Press, NY, 2002), pp. 14–15 and 60–71.

On April 19, 1861, a regiment of Union troops from Massachusetts was marching through Baltimore when a mob of Southern sympathizers attacked them with bricks, paving stones, and pistols. The troops fired back and had to fight their way through town. Four soldiers and twelve citizens were killed—the first official deaths in the Civil War. James Ryder Randall composed "My Maryland" to recall this riot, hoping it would coax Maryland into the war on the Confederate side. The complete poem can be found in Richard Marius, ed,

*The Columbia Book of Civil War Poetry: From Whitman to Walcott* (Columbia University Press, NY, 1994), pp. 59–62.

Two books discuss the shifting momentum of the war and how it shaped Lee's decision to invade the north: Shelby Foote, *The Civil War: A Narrative: Fort Sumter to Perryville* (Random House, NY, 1974); and McPherson, *Antietam*, pp. 11–34.

The use of cotton as a bargaining tool was openly discussed in the South. The editor of the Charleston *Mercury* declared, "The cards are in our hands and we intend to play them out to the bankruptcy of every cotton factory in Great Britain and France or the acknowledgment of our independence." The importance of cotton and its use in Southern diplomacy is discussed in James M. McPherson, *Battle Cry of Freedom: The Civil War Era* (Oxford University Press, NY, 1988), pp. 383–386 and 548–550; as well as Bruce Catton, *The Civil War* (American Heritage, NY, 1985), pp. 99–109.

Robert E. Lee was a brilliant military strategist as well as a charismatic leader of men. He was so highly regarded by Abraham Lincoln and General-in-Chief of the Union Armies Winfield Scott that he was offered command of the newly levied Union army in 1861. Despite feeling that slavery was "a moral and political evil," he decided he had to side with the South when Virginia voted to secede, saying "I cannot raise my hand against my birthplace, my home, my children." More can be learned about Robert E. Lee in John Esten Cooke, *Robert E. Lee* (G.W. Dillingham, NY, 1899); Clifford Dowdey, *Lee* (Little Brown, Boston, 1965); Douglas Southall Freeman, *R. E. Lee*, 4 vols. (Charles Scribner's Sons, NY, 1934–35); Gary W. Gallagher, ed., *Lee the Soldier* (Bison Books, Lincoln, NE, 1999); and John

William Jones, *Life and Letters of Robert E. Lee, Soldier and Man* (Neale Publishing, NY, 1906).

## 2. Panic

In July 1864, Confederate Major Harry Gilmore was sent to blow up railroad bridges in Maryland. Two members of his advance guard were riding through Green Spring Valley when they came upon a giant US flag flying over the road in front of Ishmael Day's house. The two demanded that Day take down the flag, and when Day refused, an argument ensued in which Day eventually shot and killed one of the men. By the time the rest of Gilmore's troops arrived, Day had escaped to a nearby field. While Elizabeth Akers Allen's poem "The Ballad of Ishmael Day" isn't about Lee's first invasion of the North, it does capture the fear many felt as an enemy approached. I found this version in Frank Moore, *The Civil War in Song and Story, 1860–1865* (P.F. Collier Publisher, NY, 1865), p. 347.

The defeat of Pope's army, McClellan's part in that defeat, and the resulting panic in Washington are discussed in McPherson, *The Battle Cry of Freedom*, pp. 524–534; and McPherson, *Antietam*, pp. 53–55 and 78–87.

A very interesting look at George B. McClellan's often difficult personality and his relationship with Abraham Lincoln and his cabinet is located in Murfin, *The Gleam of Bayonets*, pp. 33–60. Also of interest is McPherson, *Antietam*, pp. 14–16, 53–55, 80, and 84–86. Additional information about McClellan can be found in Gabor S. Boritt, ed., *Lincoln's Generals* (Oxford University Press, NY, 1995); Peter Cozzens, *General John Pope: A Life for the Nation* (University of Illinois Press, Urbana, IL, 2005); Thomas J. Rowland, *George B. McClellan and*

*Civil War History* (Kent State University Press, Kent, OH, 1998); Stephen W. Sears, *George B. McClellan: The Young Napoleon* (Da Capo Press, NY, 1999); Stephen W. Sears, *To the Gates of Richmond: The Peninsula Campaign* (Ticknor & Fields, NY, 1992); and T. Harry Williams, *Lincoln and His Generals* (Gramercy Books, NY, 2001). McClellan left his impressions of Lincoln, Pope, and Lee in George B. McClellan, *McClellan's Own Story: The War for the Union, the Soldiers Who Fought It, the Civilians Who Directed It, and His Relations to It and Them* (Charles L. Webster, NY, 1887) and in numerous letters to his wife, Ellen, which are contained in Letterbook, McClellan Papers, Manuscript Division, Library of Congress.

A concise look at Lincoln's stand on slavery and emancipation can be found in James M. McPherson, *Drawn with the Sword: Reflections on the American Civil War* (Oxford University Press, NY, 1997), pp. 192–207. Also see John Hope Franklin, *The Emancipation Proclamation* (Doubleday, Garden City, NY, 1963); Hans L. Trefousse, ed., *Lincoln's Decision for Emancipation* (Lippincott Books, Philadelphia, PA, 1975); and James M. McPherson, *Abraham Lincoln and the Second American Revolution* (Oxford University Press, NY, 1991).

Frederick Douglass's quote appeared in the *Montgomery Advertiser*, November 6, 1861.

### 3. Onwards

Father Abram Joseph Ryan was a Catholic priest whose poem uses images of brave knights fearlessly fighting for a good cause against overwhelming odds. From Marius, *The Columbia Book of Civil War Poetry*, pp. 267–268.

The logistical problems Lee faced when he entered Maryland, as well as his opinion of McClellan and his

decision to seize Harper's Ferry, are looked at in detail in Harsh, *Taken at the Flood*, pp. 71–75, 81–85, and 135–143.

Harsh also has a long section on Special Orders 191 and why Lee divided up his army, pp. 152–167. See also Sears, *Landscape Turned Red*, pp. 90, 91–92, and 104; Murfin, *The Gleam of Bayonets*, pp. 113–117; and McPherson, *Antietam*, pp. 106–109.

### 4. S.O. 191

Herman Melville published his classic whaling story, *Moby Dick*, in 1851, but it proved a critical and financial failure. By the time the Civil War began, Melville thought himself a failure as a writer. "Ball's Bluff" was written shortly after the Battle of Ball's Bluff in 1861, and was included in his *Battle Pieces and Aspects of War*, published in 1866. My version was found in Marius, *The Columbia Book of Civil War Poetry*, pp. 8–9.

McClellan provides an interesting look at the condition of the Army of the Potomac and how he reorganized it in George B. McClellan, *Report on the Organization of the Army of the Potomac, and Its Campaigns in Virginia and Maryland* (Government Printing Office, Washington, D.C., 1864). Also of value were Bruce Catton, *Mr. Lincoln's Army* (Doubleday, Garden City, NY, 1954); and Warren W. Hassler Jr., *General George McClellan: Shield of the Union* (Louisiana State University Press, Baton Rouge, LA, 1957).

Allan Pinkerton served as chief detective for the Army of the Potomac from August 1861 to November 1862. "Pinkerton was sadly out of his depth," writes historian Bruce Catton in his *The Civil War*, "through a series of fantastic miscalculations he consistently estimated Confederate numbers at double or treble their actual strength, and McClellan trusted him implicitly." See also John T. Hubbell, ed., *Battles Lost and Won: Essays from Civil War History* (Greenwood Press, Westport, CT, 1976), pp. 83–106.

The logistics of moving any army are staggering. Consider that when McClellan's army marched, it required more than 39,000 horses (which had to be fed and cared for constantly). An interesting and humorous discussion of army horses, mules, wagons, and the men who cared for them can be found in John D. Billings, *Hardtack and Coffee or the Unwritten Story of Army Life* (University of Nebraska Press, Lincoln, NE, 1993), pp. 279–297, 324–329, and 350–376.

### 5. The Gaps

Oliver Wendell Holmes wrote "To Canaan: A Puritan War Song" on August 12, 1862. I found my version in John Truesdale, *The Blue Coats, and How They Fought and Died for the Union* (Jones Brothers & Co., Philadelphia, PA, 1867), pp. 164–165.

Information about the Battle of South Mountain come from a number of sources, including Daniel Harvey Hill, "The Battle of South Mountain, or 'Boonsboro': Fighting for Time at Turner's and Fox's Gaps," from Robert Underwood Johnson and Clarence Clough Buel, eds., *North to Antietam: Battles and Leaders of the Civil War*, vol. 2, (Thomas Yoseloff, NY, 1956); pp. 559–581, John Michael Priest, *Before Antietam: The Battle for South Mountain* (White Mane Press, Shippensburg, PA, 1992); and Edward James Stackpole, *From Cedar Mountain to Antietam: August–September, 1862: Cedar Mountain, Second Manassas, Chantilly, Harpers Ferry, South Mountain, Antietam* (Stackpole Press, Harrisburg, PA, 1959).

Casualty figures in this book are really just estimates, because record-keeping on both sides was haphazard at best. No book can adequately describe how truly chaotic and confusing things are during and immediately after a major battle; officers are generally more concerned with the survival of their men than with counting the wounded and dead. In addition, soldiers often were separated from or wandered away from their companies and regiments, some to be absorbed into other units, some to go home. These men were often reported as casualties. My numbers come from a careful reading and consideration of the following sources: Thomas L. Livermore, *Numbers and Losses in the Civil War in America, 1861–1865,* updated version (Morningside Press, Dayton, OH, 1986), and a copy of an unpublished manuscript by Ezra Carman, "The Maryland Campaign of 1862" at the Antietam National Battlefield Library.

### 6. Retreat

With the war going against them in 1864, C. C. Mera wrote "No Surrender" to bolster the sagging spirits of fellow Southerners. From Abel, *Singing the New Nation*, p. 126.

After the surrender of Harper's Ferry, a court of inquiry was formed to determine what had happened there and whether Dixon Miles was at fault. Miles, who died as a result of wounds sustained during the siege, was censured, while another officer was discharged from the service. A detailed discussion of the siege of Harper's Ferry can be found in the Official Records, XIX, Part 1, pp. 549–803 (U.S. War Department, The War of the Rebellion: A Compilation of the Official Records of the Union and Confederate Armies).

Benjamin Davis's daring escape from Harper's Ferry and his wild nighttime ride is examined very nicely in

John W. Mies, "Breakout at Harper's Ferry," *Civil War History*, II, no. 2 (June 1956), pp. 13–28.

The Confederate retreat and Lee's decision to stand at Sharpsburg are examined in detail in Harsh, *Taken at the Flood*, pp. 287–297 and 301–307.

### 7. A Great Tumbling Together

Walt Whitman's "The Artilleryman's Vision" has a Civil War veteran waking in the middle of a quiet night and remembering a long-ago battle. Whitman never experienced actual battle, but his poem is one of the best descriptions of the chaos and noisy turmoil of combat. From Marius, ed., *The Columbia Book of Civil War Poetry*, pp. 174–175.

Many books were consulted in my reconstruction of the fighting on the Union right flank. They include: William C. Davis, *The Battlefields of the Civil War* (University of Oklahoma Press, Norman, OK, 2000), pp. 77–80; Harsh, *Taken at the Flood*, pp. 368–395; Frances H. Kennedy, ed., *The Civil War Battlefield Guide* (Houghton Mifflin Company, Boston, 1998), pp. 118–120; Murfin, *The Gleam of Bayonets*, pp. 213–225; John Michael Priest, *Antietam: The Soldier's Battle* (Oxford University Press, NY, 1989), 29–124; Sears, *Landscape Turned Red*, pp. 173–215; and *The Century War Book* (Century Company, NY, 1887), pp. 153.

### 8. The Sunken Road

Oliver Wendell Holmes's "Trumpet Song" appeared in Moore, *The Civil War in Song and Story*, pp. 114–115.

Discussions of the Sunken Road and the battle for the Confederate center can be located in: Davis, *The Battlefields of the Civil War*, pp. 80–81; Harsh, *Taken at the Flood*, pp. 395–397; Kennedy, ed., *The Civil War Battlefield Guide*, pp. 120; Murfin, *The Gleam of Bayonets*, pp. 226, 239–255; Priest, *Antietam*, pp. 134–146, 156–160, 169–191; Sears, *Landscape Turned Red*, pp. 216–254; *The Century War Book*, pp. 149, 152, 155.

### 9. Burnside's Bridge

One theme in John Greenleaf Whittier's "The Battle Autumn of 1862" is that in the end Nature will prevail and heal the terrible wounds of war. From Marius, ed., *Columbia Book of Civil War Poetry*, pp. 369–371.

The storming of Burnside's Bridge (also known as the Lower Bridge) are detailed in Harsh, *Taken at the Flood*, pp. 305, 345–347, 382–383, 398, 400, 406; Moore, *The Civil War in Song and Story*, pp. 476–477; Murfin, *The Gleam of Bayonets*, pp. 259–271; Sears, *Landscape Turned Red*, pp. 260–268, 276, 353–356; and Philip Thomas Tucker, *Burnside's Bridge: The Climatic Struggle of the 2nd and 20th Georgia at Antietam Creek* (Stackpole Books, Mechanicsburg, PA, 2000, pp. 69–152.

### 10. Cemetery Hill

Charles Leighton wrote this poem in 1862 as a tribute to the Union victory at Antietam. It was later set to music and can be found in The Lester S. Levy Collection of Sheet Music, Special Collections at the Sheridan Libraries of John Hopkins University.

Additional details of the afternoon fighting can be read in: Harsh, *Taken at the Flood*, pp. 413–424; Murfin, *The Gleam of Bayonets*, pp. 271–278; Priest, *Antietam*, pp. 253–309; Sears, *Landscape Turned Red*, pp. 268–297.

### 11. The Smell of Death

Severn Teackle Wallis was a lawyer and a Maryland Quaker who opposed slavery and secession, but was also against using force to suppress it. As a result he was arrested in 1861 and spent a year in jail. From Marius, ed., *The Columbia Book of Civil War Poetry*, pp. 3–5.

Information about the medical treatment of the wounded and the burial of the dead came from George Worthington Adams, *Doctors in Blue: The Medical History of the Union Army in the Civil War* (Louisiana State University Press, Baton Rouge, LA, 1952), pp. 65, 76–79; H. H. Cunningham, *Doctors in Gray: The Confederate Medical Service* (Louisiana State University Press, Baton Rouge, LA, 1958), pp. 129–133, 175; Philip Katcher, *The Civil War Source Book* (Facts, Inc., NY, 1995), pp. 86–87, 120–122, 173–176, 198–201; Sears, *Landscape Turned Red*, pp. 304–306; Priest, *Antietam*, pp. 309–316. It should be noted that the work of caring for the wounded and burying the dead was so overwhelming that even months later the landscape was still littered with bodies. A Confederate private from Virginia on his way to Gettysburg in June 1863 stopped by Sharpsburg and wrote home:

Dear Father Mother and Family,

I have been this morning over the old Sharpsburg battle field and have witnessed the most horrible sights that my eyes ever beheld I saw dead Yankees in any numbers just lying on top of the ground with a little dirt throwed over them and hogs rooting them out of the ground and eating them and others lying on top of the ground with the flesh picked off and their bones bleaching and they by many hundreds! Oh what a horrible sight for human beings to look upon in a civilized Country! When will this horrible war ever end. . . . G. K. Harlow

In addition to Galloway, at least one other woman was wounded while fighting at Antietam. Catherine Davidson was shot in the right arm. After the battle, Davidson was carried to an ambulance by Pennsylvania Governor Curtin, who had no idea Davidson was a woman. Davidson believed she was dying and gave Curtin her ring as a gesture of thanks for his kindness. Davidson survived, but lost her arm when surgeons amputated it halfway between the shoulder and elbow. Later, Davidson, dressed now as a woman, met Curtin and told the surprised governor who she was. Curtin, who had worn the ring since that day at Antietam, offered it back to her, but Davidson refused, saying, "The finger that used to wear that ring will never wear it again. The hand is dead, but the soldier still lives." For more details on Galloway, Davidson, and other women involved in the battle, see Stephen B. Oates, *A Woman of Valor: Clara Barton and the Civil War* (Free Press, NY, 1994), pp. 91–93, 97–98; and Elizabeth Brown Pryor, *Clara Barton: Professional Angel* (University of Pennsylvania Press, Philadelphia, PA, 1987), p. 99.

The confrontation between Abraham Lincoln and George McClellan following the battle is very nicely summed up in McPherson, *Antietam*, pp. 133–156; Murfin, *The Gleam of Bayonets*, pp. 299–316; Sears, *Landscape Turned Red*, pp. 306–317, 323–332, 336–345.

The photographic work of Alexander Gardner and James F. Gibson is covered in depth in William A. Frassanito, *Antietam: The Photographic Legacy of America's Bloodiest Day* (Charles Scribner's Sons, NY, 1978).

Francis Miles Finch wrote "The Blue and the Gray" in 1867 as an ode to healing the rift between the North and the South. It quickly became one of the most famous poems to come out of the Civil War. From Marius, ed., *The Columbia Book of the Civil War*, pp. 410–413.

## 12. Emancipation

Ralph Waldo Emerson was against slavery, but at first he opposed the aggressive language of some abolitionists, such as William Lloyd Garrison. His attitude changed after the passage of the Fugitive Slave Law in 1850 (which required the return of all slaves who had escaped to the North). He read "Boston Hymn" on the day the Emancipation Proclamation went into effect. From Marius, ed., *The Columbia Book of Civil War Poetry*, pp. 75–78.

Several fine books were consulted regarding the Emancipation Proclamation, including Franklin, *The Emancipation Proclamation*; Trefousse, ed., *Lincoln's Decision for Emancipation*; Benjamin Quarles, *Lincoln and the Negro* (Da Capo Press, NY, 1991); and McPherson, *Abraham Lincoln and the Second American Revolution*. Frederick Douglass's praise for the Emancipation Proclamation appeared in *Douglass' Monthly*, (October 1862), p. 721.

While neither side allowed African-American men to be soldiers in 1861, the Union navy had several thousand African-American sailors from the very start of the conflict. Even after being allowed to serve in the Union army, African-American soldiers received lower pay, and despite valiant service, none rose above the rank of major. Ironically, as Confederate fortunes declined, some Southerners urged that African-American forces be used to fight the North. General Patrick Cleburne suggested in January 1864 that slaves be armed to fight for the Confederacy and freed on completion of duty. His idea was suppressed for a number of months, but eventually the Confederate Congress approved it in March, 1865. A company of African-American Confederate soldiers was organized and did drill in Richmond's main square, but the war ended before they were able to enter combat. For more on African Americans in the military, see William C. Davis, ed., *Touched by Fire: A National Historical Society Photographic Portrait of the Civil War* (Black Dog & Leventhal Publishers, NY, 1997), pp. 48, 187, 235, 276, 350, 414, 513–514, and 524–532.

# A BIBLIOGRAPHY OF VOICES

❖

This book contains first-person extracts from many individuals. These voices come from a great many sources, a number of which are listed below. Several have already been cited, but contain additional material about the Battle of Antietam, plus details about the soldiers' emotions, army life, and officers.

J. Gregory Acken, ed., *Inside the Army of the Potomac: The Civil War Experience of Captain Francis Adams Donaldson* (Stackpole Books, Mechanicsburg, PA, 1998).

*The Annals of the War, Written by Leading Participants, North and South, Originally Published in the Philadelphia Weekly Times* (Times Publishing Co., Philadelphia, 1879).

John D. Billings, *Hardtack & Coffee or The Unwritten Story of Army Life* (University of Nebraska Press, Lincoln, NE, 1993).

Robert Goldthwaite Carter, *Four Brothers in Blue or Sunshine and Shadows of the War of the Rebellion: A Story of the Great Civil War from Bull Run to Appomattox* (University of Oklahoma Press, Norman, OK, 1999).

*The Century War Book* (Century Co., NY, 1885).

Henry Steele Commager, ed., *The Blue and the Gray: The Story of the Civil War as Told by Participants*, vol. 1 (The Bobbs-Merrill Company, Inc., Indianapolis, IN, 1950).

Burke Davis, ed., *I Rode with Jeb Stuart: The Life and Campaigns of Major General J. E. B. Stuart* (Houghton Mifflin, Boston, 1885).

Charles E. Davis, *Three Years in the Army: The Story of the Thirteenth Massachusetts Volunteers* (Estes & Lauriat, Boston, 1894).

Rufus R. Dawes, *Service with the Sixth Wisconsin Volunteers* (E. R. Alderman & Sons, Marietta, OH, 1890).

Henry Kyd Douglas, *I Rode with Stonewall: Being Chiefly the War Experiences of the Youngest Member of Jackson's Staff from the John Brown Raid to the Hanging of Mrs. Surrett* (University of North Carolina Press, Chapel Hill, NC, 1940).

Joseph T. Durkin, *John Dooley: Confederate Soldier* (Georgetown University Press, Washington, D.C., 1945).

S. Emma E. Edmonds, *Nurse and Spy in the Union Army* (W.S. Williams & Co., Hartford, 1865).

Mark De Wolfe Howe, ed., *Touched with Fire: Civil War Letters of Oliver Wendell Holmes Jr., 1861–1864* (Cambridge, MA, 1964).

Robert Underwood Johnson and Clarence Clough Buel, ed., *North to Antietam: Battles and Leaders of the Civil War*, vol. 2 (Thomas Yoseloff, NY, 1956).

Thomas L. A. Livermore, *Days and Events, 1860–1866* (Houghton Mifflin Co., Boston, 1920).

James Longstreet, *From Manassas to Appomattox* (Lippincott, Philadelphia, PA, 1896).

Jerome M. Loving, ed., *Civil War Letters of George Washington Whitman* (Duke University Press, Durham, NC, 1975).

Mark Nickerson, "Recollections of the Civil War by a High Private in the Front Ranks," (an unpublished manuscript in the U.S. Army Military History Institute, Carlisle Barracks, Carlisle, PA).

W. S. Nye, ed., *The Valiant Hours* (Harrisburg, PA, 1961).

Charles Phillips and Alan Axelrod, *My Brother's Face: Portraits of the Civil War in Photographs, Diaries, and Letters* (Chronicle Books, San Francisco, 1993).

Marcia Reid-Green, ed., *Letters Home: Henry Matrau of the Iron Brigade* (University of Nebraska Press, Lincoln, NE, 1993).

James I. Robertson, ed., *Four Years With General Lee* (Bloomington, IL, 1962).

Emil and Ruth Rosenblatt, eds., *Hard Marching Every Day: The Civil War Letters of Private Wilbur Fisk, 1861–1865* (Lawrence, KS, 1992).

G. Moxley Sorrel, *Recollections of a Confederate Staff Officer* (Neale, NY, 1905).

D. H. Strother, "Personal Recollections of the War, By a Virginian," *Harper's New Monthly Magazine*, XXXVI (1868).

Byrd Barnette Tribble, ed., *Benjamin Cason Rawlings: First Virginia Volunteer for the South* (Butternut and Blue, Baltimore, 1996).

Robert J. Trout, *With Pen and Saber: The Letters and Diaries of J.E.B. Stuart's Staff Officers* (Stackpole Books, Mechanicsburg, PA, 1995).

Captain John Truesdale, *The Blue Coats and How They Lived, Fought and Died for the Union* (Jones Brothers & Co., Philadelphia, 1867).

Richard Wheeler, ed., *Lee's Terrible Swift Sword: From Antietam to Chancellorsville: An Eyewitness History* (NY, 1992).

Alpheus S. Williams, *From the Cannon's Mouth: The Civil War Letters of Alpheus S. Williams* (Detroit, 1959).
Abolition, 14

# INDEX